Form & Function
MODERN GANSEYS
>>>><<<< *by Knit Picks* >>>><<<<

Copyright 2019 © Knit Picks

All rights reserved. This book or any portion thereof may not be reproduced or used in any manner whatsoever without the express written permission of the publisher except for the use of brief quotations in a book review.

Photography by John Cranford

Printed in the United States of America

First Printing, 2019

ISBN 978-1-62767-248-1

Versa Press, Inc.
800-447-7829

www.versapress.com

CONTENTS

What's a Gansey?   7

Aberdovey *by Theresa Shingler*   8

Barnstaple Vest *by Sandi Rosner*   16

Double Cross Pullover *by Adrienne Larsen*   24

Empire *by Kirsten Joel*   36

Gray Days *by Hope Vickman*   42

Jetty *by Renate Kamm*   54

Olympic Pullover *by Allison Griffith*   62

Pleinmont *by Bridget Pupillo*   70

Sandy Road *by Beverley Dott*   82

St. Martin's Guernsey *by Donna Estin*   90

Glossary   100

What's a Gansey?

A gansey, which may also be called a guernsey—the words are interchangeable—is a traditional kind of handknit pullover worn by British herring fisherman in the 19th and early 20th centuries. Classic ganseys were cream or navy colored, knit seamlessly with dropped shoulders, and were made to be extremely practical for the wearers. Warm, water-resistant, and easy to move around in, ganseys were the perfect garments for hardworking fishermen.

True ganseys are very tightly knit, using densely twisted, 5-ply, sport weight wool, on size US 1 or 2 needles, making a nearly waterproof fabric that shows off knit/purl textured patterns beautifully. While the patterns in this book are inspired by these traditional garments, they use more modern (and pleasant to knit) gauges.

Ganseys are always made in just one solid color and feature textured patterning either throughout or only on the top (the yoke) of the sweater. Traditional patterns range in complexity, consist of knit stitches, purl stitches, and sometimes cables, and the front and back of a gansey are always patterned the same. In fact, it was common for the front and back of a classic gansey to be exactly the same, so that the wearer could reverse which way it was worn, extending the life of the garment.

Traditional gansey construction is in the round, from the bottom up to the armholes, where the front and back are separated and each worked flat; the shoulders are then joined, and the collar and sleeves are each worked in the round from picked-up stitches. The projects in this collection vary; some use traditional construction—one even includes the classic gansey gusset under the arms—and some use different kinds of processes, styles, and contemporary sweater shapes.

ABERDOVEY

by Theresa Shingler

FINISHED MEASUREMENTS
31.5 (35, 38.75, 45.75, 47.5, 51, 54.75, 60, 63.5)" finished chest circumference; meant to be worn with 2-3" positive ease

YARN
Knit Picks Simply Wool™ (worsted weight, 100% Eco Wool; 218 yards/100g): Wendy 27469, 6 (7, 8, 9, 9, 10, 11, 12, 12) hanks

NEEDLES
US 8 (5mm) 24" or longer circular needles, or size to obtain gauge

NOTIONS
Yarn Needle
Stitch Markers
Cable Needle

GAUGE
18 sts and 26 rows = 4" in Stockinette Stitch, blocked

For pattern support, contact theresashinglerknits@gmail.com

Aberdovey

Notes:

The Aberdovey gansey is very much inspired by the traditional fishing ganseys knit up and down the coasts of the UK and worn by hard-working fishermen.

The front and back have the same patterning at the chest area. The shoulder gives the appearance of a traditional dropped shoulder, but there is a little shaping both in the body and in the sleeve head to make it easier to wear. The neck is picked up and worked once the shoulders are seamed together. The sleeves have the same cross/diamond pattern running up them as runs up the center of the chest.

Charts are worked flat; read RS rows (odd numbers) from right to left, and WS rows (even numbers) from left to right.

DIRECTIONS

Sleeves (make two the same)

Sleeve is worked flat from the wrist up.
CO 37 (41, 45, 45, 49, 53, 61, 65, 69) sts.
Rows 1-4: K across.
Row 5 (WS): (P3, K1) to last st, P1.
Row 6 (RS): K1, (P1, K3) to end.
Rows 7-10: Rep Rows 5-6 two more times.
Row 11: Rep Row 5.
Row 12-15: K across.
Row 16: K10 (12, 14, 12, 14, 16, 18, 20, 22), PM, work first row of Central & Sleeve Motif chart as indicated for your size, PM, K10 (12, 14, 12, 14, 16, 18, 20, 22).
Row 17: P to M, SM, work next row of Central & Sleeve Motif chart, SM, P to end.
Inc Row: K2, MIR, K to M, SM, work next row of Central & Sleeve Motif chart, SM, K to last 2 sts, MIL, K2. 2 sts inc.
39 (43, 47, 47, 51, 55, 63, 67, 71) sts.

Working Central & Sleeve Motif chart as established, rep Inc Row every 4 (4, 4, 4, 2, 2, 2, 2, 2) rows 10 (10, 10, 14, 15, 16, 16, 17, 19) more times. 59 (63, 67, 75, 81, 87, 95, 101, 109) sts. Cont without incs until work measures 16 (15.25, 14.75, 14.75, 14.25, 14, 13, 12.75, 11.75)" from CO edge.

Short Row Upper Arm Shaping

Short Row 1: Work as established to 5 sts from end, W&T.
Short Row 2: Work as established to 5 sts from end, W&T.

Sizes 38.75"-63.5" Only

Short Row 3: Work as established to 5 sts from previous wrapped st, W&T.
Short Row 4: Work as established to 5 sts from previous wrapped st, W&T.

Sizes 47.5"-63.5" Only

Short Row 5: Rep Short Row 3.
Short Row 6: Rep Short Row 4.

Sizes 54.75"-63.5" Only

Short Row 7: Rep Short Row 3.
Short Row 8: Rep Short Row 4.

Sleeve Cap Shaping

All sizes resume.
Row 1: Work as established to end, picking up and working wraps.
Row 2: Work as established to end, picking up and working wraps.
Row 3: K1, SSK, work to last 3 sts, K2tog, K1. 2 sts dec.

Sizes 38.75"-63.5" Only

Work even in pattern for three rows.

Sizes 47.5"-63.5" Only

Row 7: Rep Row 3. 2 sts dec.
Work even in pattern for two rows.

Sizes 54.75"-63.5" Only

Work even in pattern for three rows.

57 (61, 65, 73, 77, 83, 91, 97, 105) sts.
BO remaining sts.

Back

Worked from the hem up.
CO 73 (81, 89, 105, 109, 117, 125, 137, 145) sts.
Rows 1-4: K across.
Row 5 (WS): (P3, K1) to last st, P1.
Row 6 (RS): K1, (P1, K3) to end.
Rows 7-12: Rep Rows 5-6 three more times.
Row 13: Rep Row 5.
Rows 14-18: K across.
Row 19: P across.
Cont in St st until work measures 9 (9, 9, 9, 9.5, 9.5, 9.5, 9.5, 9.5)" from CO edge, ending on a RS row.

Patterned Chest

Knit three rows.
Setup Row 1 (RS): K3 (7, 11, 16, 20, 24, 26, 32, 36), PM, P1, K7, KFB, PM, K7 (7, 7, 8, 6, 6, 6, 6, 6), PM, work first row of Central & Sleeve Motif chart as indicated for your size, PM, K7 (7, 7, 8, 6, 6, 6, 6, 6), PM, P1, K7, KFB, PM, K3 (7, 11, 16, 20, 24, 26, 32, 36). 2 sts inc.
Setup Row 2 (WS): P to M, SM, K1, P8, K1, SM, P to M, SM, work next row of Central & Sleeve Motif chart, SM, P to M, SM, K1, P8, K1, SM, P to end.
Row 1: K to M, SM, work Row 1 of Side Cable chart, SM, K to M, SM, work next row of Central & Sleeve Motif chart, SM, K to M, SM, work Row 1 of Side Cable chart, SM, K to end.
Row 2: P to M, SM, work next row of Side Cable chart, SM, P to M, SM, work next row of Central & Sleeve Motif chart, SM, P to M, SM, work next row of Side Cable chart, SM, P to end.
Cont to work charts as established until work measures 18 (18, 18, 18, 19, 19, 19, 19, 19)" from CO edge, ending on a WS row.

Underarm Shaping

Row 1 (RS): K1, SSK, work as established to last 3 sts, K2tog, K1. 2 sts dec.
Row 2 (WS): Work across as established.

Rep Rows 1-2 0 (0, 1, 1, 2, 2, 3, 3, 3) more times. 2 (2, 4, 4, 6, 6, 8, 8, 8) sts dec. 73 (81, 87, 103, 105, 113, 119, 131, 139) sts.

**Cont to work charts as established until work measures 22 (22.5, 23, 23.75, 25.5, 25.75, 26.5, 27.25, 28)" from CO edge, ending with a WS row.

Back neck shaping
In patterns as established, work 18 (22, 25, 32, 33, 37, 39, 45, 49) sts, BO 37 (37, 37, 39, 39, 39, 41, 41, 41) sts, work to end. 18 (22, 25, 32, 33, 37, 39, 45, 49) sts each shoulder.

Left Shoulder
Row 1 (WS): Work across as established.
Row 2 (RS): K1, SSK, work to end.
Rep Rows 1-2 5 (5, 5, 5, 5, 5, 6, 6, 6) more times. 12 (16, 19, 26, 27, 31, 32, 38, 42) sts.
Work even as established for 0 (0, 0, 0, 0, 4, 2, 2, 2) rows.

Short row shaping
Row 1 (WS): Work across as established.
Short Row 2 (RS): Work 6 (9, 10, 14, 15, 15, 18, 22, 24) sts, W&T.
Short Row 3: Work to end.
Short Row 4: Work 3 (4, 5, 7, 7, 7, 9, 11, 12) sts, W&T.
Short Row 5: Work to end.
BO all sts.

Right Shoulder
Join yarn at shoulder edge.
Row 1 (RS): Work to last 3 sts, K2tog, K1.
Row 2 (WS): Work to end.
Rep Rows 1-2 5 (5, 5, 5, 5, 5, 6, 6, 6) more times. 12 (16, 19, 26, 27, 31, 32, 38, 42) sts.
Work even as established for 1 (1, 1, 1, 5, 3, 3, 3) rows.

Short row shaping
Short Row 1 (WS): Work 6 (9, 10, 14, 15, 15, 18, 22, 24) sts, W&T.
Short Row 2 (RS): Work to end.
Short Row 3: Work 3 (4, 5, 7, 7, 7, 9, 11, 12) sts, W&T.
Short Row 4: Work to end.
Row 5: Work across as established.
BO all sts.

Front
Work as for Back until **.
Cont to work charts as established until work measures 19.5 (20, 19.5, 20.25, 22, 21.75, 22.5, 23.25, 24)" from CO edge, ending with a WS row.

Front Neck Shaping
In patterns as established, work 24 (28, 31, 39, 40, 44, 46, 52, 56) sts, BO 25 (25, 25, 25, 25, 25, 27, 27, 27) sts, work to end. 24 (28, 31, 39, 40, 44, 46, 52, 56) sts each shoulder.

Right Shoulder
Row 1 (WS): Work across as established.
Row 2 (RS): K1, SSK, work to end.
Rep Rows 1-2 11 (11, 11, 12, 12, 12, 13, 13, 13) more times.
Work even as established for 4 (4, 12, 10, 10, 16, 14, 14, 14) rows.

Short row shaping
Row 1 (WS): Work across as established.
Short Row 2 (RS): Work 6 (9, 10, 14, 15, 15, 18, 22, 24), W&T.
Short Row 3: Work to end.
Short Row 4: Work 3 (4, 5, 7, 7, 7, 9, 11, 12), W&T.
Short Row 5: Work to end.
BO all sts.

Left Shoulder
Join yarn at shoulder edge.
Row 1 (RS): Work to last three sts K2tog, K1.
Row 2 (WS): Work across as established.
Rep Rows 1-2 11 (11, 11, 12, 12, 12, 13, 13, 13) more times.
Work even as established for 5 (5, 13, 11, 11, 17, 15, 15, 15) rows.

Short row shaping
Short Row 1 (WS): Work 6 (9, 10, 14, 15, 15, 18, 22, 24), W&T.
Short Row 2 (RS): Work to end.
Short Row 3: Work 3 (4, 5, 7, 7, 7, 9, 11, 12), W&T.
Short Row 4: Work to end.
Row 5: Work across as established.
BO all sts.

Neckline
Seam shoulders.
With RS facing, PU and K 37 (37, 37, 39, 39, 39, 41, 41, 41) sts across back neck, 33 (33, 39, 38, 38, 46, 46, 46, 46) sts down side neck, 25 (25, 25, 25, 25, 25, 27, 27, 27) sts across front neck, and 33 (33, 39, 38, 38, 46, 46, 46, 46) sts up side neck, join in the rnd. 128 (128, 140, 140, 140, 156, 160, 160, 160) sts.
Rnd 1: P all.
Rnd 2: K all.
Rnd 3: P all.
Rnd 4: K all.
Rnd 5: (K3, P1) to end.
Rnds 6-11: Rep Rnd 5, six more times.
Rnd 12: K0 (0, 4, 4, 4, 4, 0, 0, 0), (K6, K2tog) to end. 112 (112, 123, 123, 123, 137, 140, 140, 140) sts.
Rnd 13: P all.
Rnd 14: K all.
BO P-wise.

Finishing
Seam sleeves into armscye. Seam side and underarm seams. Weave in ends. Wash and block to diagram.

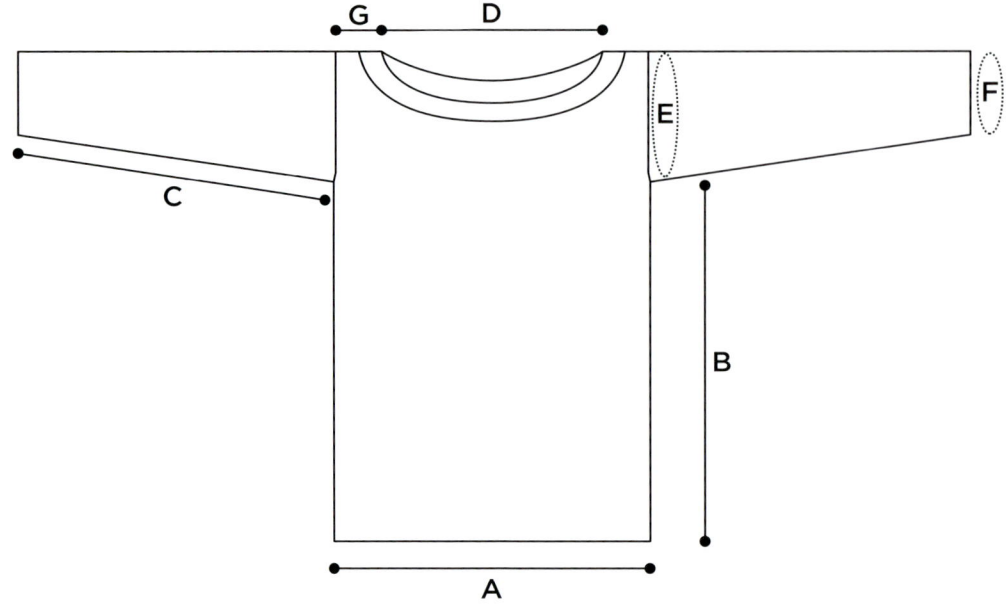

A 15.75 (17.5, 19.25, 23, 23.75, 25.5, 27.25, 30, 31.75)"

B 18 (18, 18, 18, 19, 19, 19, 19, 19)"

C 16 (15.25, 14.75, 14.75, 14.25, 14, 13, 12.75, 11.75)"

D 11 (11, 11, 11.25, 11.25, 11.25, 12.25, 12.25, 12.25)"

E 13 (14, 15, 16.75, 18, 19.25, 21, 22.5, 24.25)"

F 8.25 (9, 10, 10, 11, 11.75, 13.5, 14.5, 15.25)"

G 2.75 (3.5, 4.25, 5.75, 6, 7, 7, 8.5, 9.25)"

LEGEND

K
RS: Knit stitch
WS: Purl stitch

P
RS: Purl stitch
WS: Knit stitch

Cable 2 Over 2 Right (2/2 RC)
Sl2 to CN, hold in back; K2, K2 from CN

Cable 2 Over 2 Left (2/2 LC)
Sl2 to CN, hold in front; K2, K2 from CN

- Central Motif Sizes 56-64
- Central Motif Sizes 48 & 52
- Central Motif Sizes 32-44
- Sleeve Motif Sizes 56-62
- Sleeve Motif Sizes 44-52
- Sleeve Motif Sizes 32-40

Side Cable

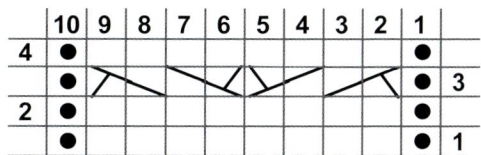

Central & Sleeve Motif

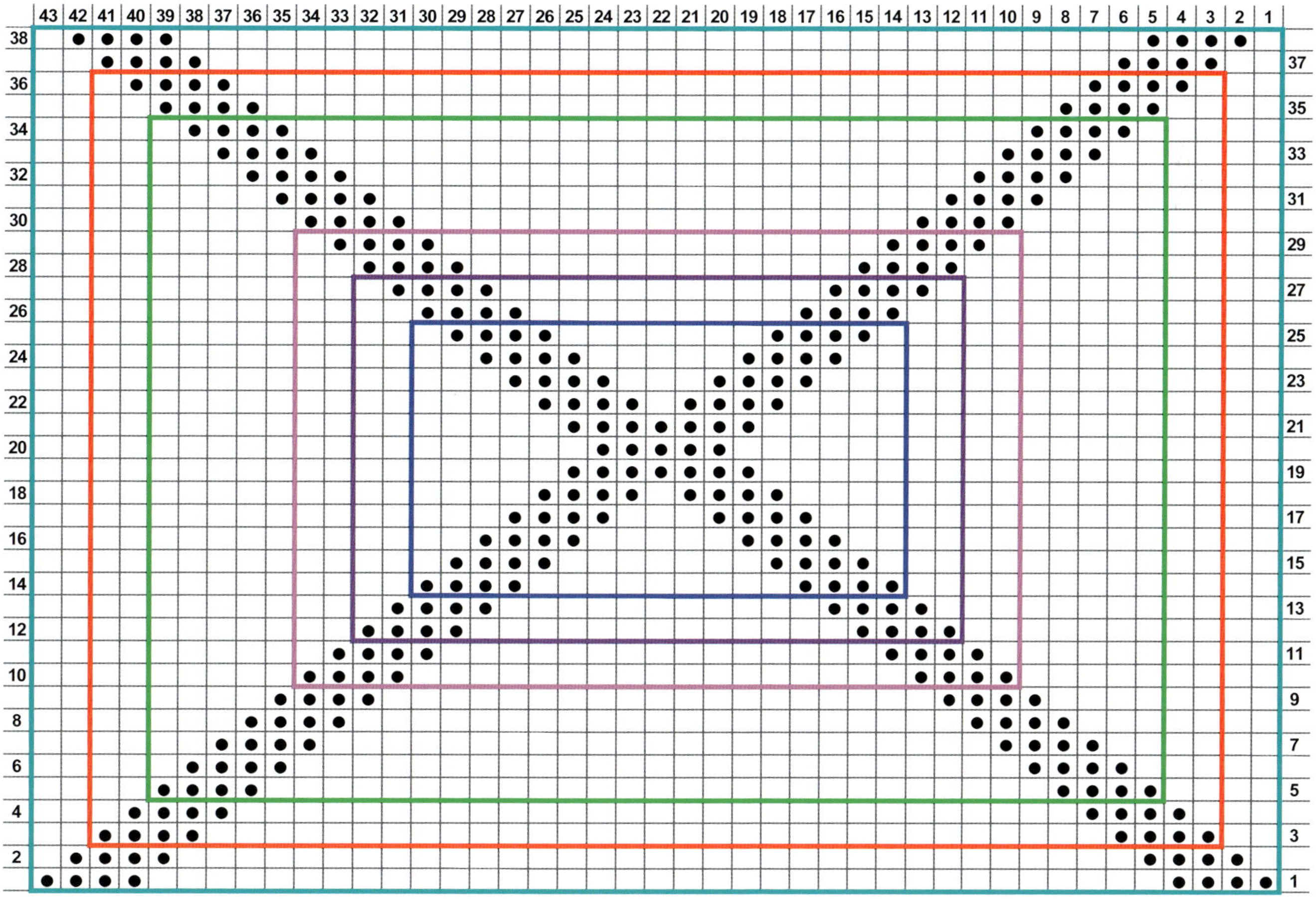

Aberdovey

BARNSTAPLE VEST

by Sandi Rosner

FINISHED MEASUREMENTS
35.75 (38.75, 41.75, 45, 48, 51.25, 54.25)" finished chest circumference; meant to be worn with 2" positive ease

YARN
Knit Picks Wool of the Andes™ (worsted weight, 100% Peruvian Highland Wool; 110 yards/50g): Persimmon Heather 24280, 6 (7, 7, 8, 9, 10, 10) skeins

NEEDLES
US 8 (5mm) 32" circular needles, or size to obtain gauge
US 6 (4mm) 16" and 32" circular needles, or two sizes smaller than size used to obtain gauge

NOTIONS
Yarn Needle
Scrap Yarn or Stitch Holder
Seven Buttons, .75" in diameter

GAUGE
18 sts and 29 rows = 4" in Double Moss Stitch Pattern, blocked

For pattern support, contact rosnersandi@gmail.com

Barnstaple Vest

Notes:
Suitable for men or women, this button-front vest will add timeless warmth to your everyday shirt and jeans. The simple, elegant textures produced by knit/purl combinations have inspired knitters for generations. This vest uses three such textures in horizontal bands to make a classic layering piece that will be welcome in any wardrobe.

The Barnstaple Vest is knit in one piece from the bottom up. All edges are trimmed with 2x2 Rib. Instructions are included for both right-over-left (traditional for women) and left-over-right (traditional for men) buttoning.

Stitch patterns are written and charted. Charts are worked flat; read RS rows (odd numbers) from right to left, and WS rows (even numbers) from left to right.

2x2 Rib (flat over a multiple of 4 sts)
Row 1 (WS): P3, (K2, P2) to last st, P1.
Row 2 (RS): K3, (P2, K2) to last st, K1.
Rep Rows 1-2 for pattern.

Marriage Lines Pattern (flat over a multiple of 14 sts plus 3)
Row 1 (RS): K across.
Row 2 (WS): P1, (P1, K1, P11, K1) to last 2 sts, P2.
Row 3: K1, P1, (K1, P1, K9, P1, K1, P1) to last st, K1.
Row 4: P1, (P1, K1, P1, K1, P7, K1, P1, K1) to last 2 sts, P2.
Row 5: K2, (K1, P1, K1, P1, K5, P1, K1, P1, K2) to last st, K1.
Row 6: P1, (P3, K1, P1, K1, P3, K1, P1, K1, P2) to last 2 sts, P2.
Row 7: K2, (K3, [P1, K1] three times, P1, K4) to last st, K1.
Row 8: P1, (P5, K1, P1, K1, P1, K1, P4) to last 2 sts, P2.
Row 9: K2, (K5, P1, K1, P1, K6) to last st, K1.
Row 10: P across.

Double Moss Stitch Pattern (flat over a multiple of 4 sts plus 1)
Row 1 (RS): K across.
Row 2 (WS): P1, (P2, K2) to last 4 sts, P2, K1, P1.
Row 3: K1, P1, (K2, P2) to last 3 sts, K3.
Row 4: P1, (K2, P2) to end.
Row 5: (K2, P2) to last st, K1.
Rows 6-13: Rep Rows 2-5 two more times.
Row 14: P across.

Double Moss Stitch Pattern (flat over a multiple of 4 sts plus 3)
Row 1 (RS): K across.
Row 2 (WS): P1, (P2, K2) to last 2 sts, P2.
Row 3: (K2, P2) to last 3 sts, K3.
Row 4: P1, (K2, P2) to 2 sts, K1, P1.
Row 5: K1, P1, (K2, P2) to last st, K1.
Rows 6-13: Rep Rows 2-5 two more times.
Row 14: P across.

Diamond Pattern (flat over a multiple of 14 sts plus 3)
Row 1 (RS): K across.
Row 2 (WS): P1, (P7, K1, P6) to last 2 sts, P2.
Row 3: K2, (K5, P1, K1, P1, K6) to last st, K1.
Row 4: P1, (P5, K1, P3, K1, P4) to last 2 sts, P2.
Row 5: K2, (K3, P1, K5, P1, K4) to last st, K1.
Row 6: P1, (P3, K1, P7, K1, P2) to last 2 sts, P2.
Row 7: K2, (K1, P1, K9, P1, K2) to last st, K1.
Row 8: P1, (P1, K1, P11, K1) to last 2 sts, P2.
Row 9: K1, P1, (K13, P1) to last st, K1.
Row 10: Rep Row 8.
Row 11: Rep Row 7.
Row 12: Rep Row 6.
Row 13: Rep Row 5.
Row 14: Rep Row 4.
Row 15: Rep Row 3.
Row 16: Rep Row 2.

DIRECTIONS

Body
Using smaller 32" circular needles, CO 156 (168, 184, 196, 212, 224, 240) sts.
Work 2x2 Rib for 14 rows, ending with a RS row.
Change to larger circular needles.
Next row (WS): P to end, increasing 1 (3, 1, 3, 1, 3, 1) sts evenly across. 157 (171, 185, 199, 213, 227, 241) sts.

Texture Stripes
Row 1 (RS): P across.
Row 2 (WS): K across.
Rows 3-12: Work Marriage Lines Pattern.
Row 13: P across.
Row 14: K across.
Rows 15-28: Work Double Moss Stitch Pattern. Note that sizes 35.75", 41.75", 48", and 54.25" are worked over a multiple of 4 sts plus 1, while sizes 38.75", 45", and 51.25" are worked over a multiple of 4 sts plus 3.
Row 29: P across.
Row 30: K across.
Rows 31-46: Work Diamond Pattern.
Row 47: P across.
Row 48: K across.
Rows 49-62: Work Double Moss Stitch Pattern.
Rep Rows 1-62 until piece measures 16 (16, 16, 16, 16, 16.5, 17)" from CO edge, ending with a WS row.

Separate Back and Front
Next Row (RS): Continuing Texture Stripes as established, work 34 (36, 39, 42, 45, 48, 51) sts in pattern for Right Front and put on holder, BO 11 (13, 15, 15, 17, 17, 19) sts for armhole, work 67 (73, 77, 85, 89, 97, 101) sts in pattern for Back and put on holder, BO 11 (13, 15, 15, 17, 17, 19) sts for armhole, work in pattern to end. 34 (36, 39, 42, 45, 48, 51) sts remain for Left Front.

Left Front
Maintain Texture Stripes pattern as established throughout.
Shape Armholes and Front Neck
Row 1 (WS): Work in pattern to end.
Row 2 (RS): K1, SSK, work in pattern to last 3 sts, K2tog, K1. 2 sts dec.
Row 3: Work in pattern to end.
Cont as established, decreasing with SSK at armhole edge every RS row 4 (6, 7, 10, 10, 11, 11) more times.
AT THE SAME TIME, dec with K2tog at neck edge every RS row 4 (3, 4, 3, 7, 5, 7) more times, then every fourth row 11 (12, 13, 14, 13, 15, 15) times.
When armhole and neck shaping are complete, 13 (13, 13, 13, 13, 15, 16) sts remain.
Work even in pattern until armhole measures 8 (8.5, 9, 9.5, 10, 10.5, 11)", ending with a WS row.
BO all sts.

Right Front
Place Right Front sts on needle. Join yarn at armhole edge. Maintain Texture Stripes pattern as established throughout.
Shape Armholes and Front Neck
Row 1 (WS): Work in pattern to end.
Row 2 (RS): K1, SSK, work in pattern to last 3 sts, K2tog, K1. 2 sts dec.
Row 3: Work in pattern to end.
Cont as established, decreasing with K2tog at armhole edge every RS row 4 (6, 7, 10, 10, 11, 11) more times.
AT THE SAME TIME, dec with SSK at neck edge every RS row 4 (3, 4, 3, 7, 5, 7) more times, then every fourth row 11 (12, 13, 14, 13, 15, 15) times.
When armhole and neck shaping are complete, 13 (13, 13, 13, 13, 15, 16) sts remain.
Work even in pattern until armhole measures 8 (8.5, 9, 9.5, 10, 10.5, 11)", ending with a WS row.
BO all sts.

Back
Place Back sts on needle. Join yarn at left armhole edge. Maintain Texture Stripes pattern as established throughout.
Shape Armholes
Row 1 (WS): Work in pattern to end.
Row 2 (RS): K1, SSK, work in pattern to last 3 sts, K2tog, K1. 2 sts dec.
Row 3: Work in pattern to end.
Cont as established, decreasing at beginning and end of every RS row 4 (6, 7, 10, 10, 11, 11) more times. 57 (59, 61, 63, 67, 73, 77) sts remain.
Work even in pattern until armhole measures 7 (7.5, 8, 8.5, 9, 9.5, 10)", ending with a WS row.

Shape Back Neck
Row 1 (RS): Work 12 (12, 12, 12, 12, 14, 15) sts in pattern, K2tog, K1, join another ball of yarn and BO center 27 (29, 31, 33, 37, 39, 41) sts, K1, SSK, work in pattern to end. 14 (14, 14, 14, 14, 16, 17) sts each side.
Work both sides at once with separate balls of yarn.

Row 2 (WS): Work in pattern to neck edge; on other side, work in pattern to end.
Row 3: Work in pattern until 3 sts before neck edge, K2tog, K1; on other side, K1, SSK, work in pattern to end. 13 (13, 13, 13, 13, 15, 16) sts each side.
Work even in pattern until reaching same length at fronts.
BO all sts.

Finishing
Sew shoulder seams.

Armbands (make two the same)
Using 16" circular needles, PU and K 80 (84, 92, 96, 100, 104, 112) sts evenly around armhole. PM for beginning of rnd.
Work 2x2 Rib for six rnds.
BO all sts.

Front Band
Using smaller 32" circular needles, PU and K 120 (123, 125, 128, 130, 135, 140) sts along Left Front edge to shoulder, 36 (38, 38, 40, 44, 46, 48) sts along Back neck edge, and 120 (123, 125, 128, 130, 135, 140) sts along Right Front edge. 276 (284, 288, 296, 304, 316, 328) sts.
Work 2x2 Rib for three rows.
Buttonhole Row for Right-Over-Left Buttoning (traditional for women) (RS): K3, P2, (K1, SSK, YO, K2tog, K1, P2, K2, P2) seven times, work in established Rib to end.
Buttonhole Row for Left-Over-Right Buttoning (traditional for men) (RS): Work in established Rib to last 83 sts, (K1, SSK, YO, K2tog, K1, P2, K2, P2) six times, K1, SSK, YO, K2tog, K1, P2, K3.
Next row (WS): Work in established Rib, working KFB into each YO of previous row to complete buttonholes.
Work 2x2 Rib for two rows.
BO all sts.

Sew buttons to front band to correspond with buttonholes.
Weave in ends.
Block to finished measurements. Note that measurements on schematic exclude the armhole edgings and front band.

LEGEND

☐ K
RS: Knit stitch
WS: Purl stitch

• P
RS: Purl stitch
WS: Knit stitch

☐ Pattern Repeat

Marriage Lines Pattern

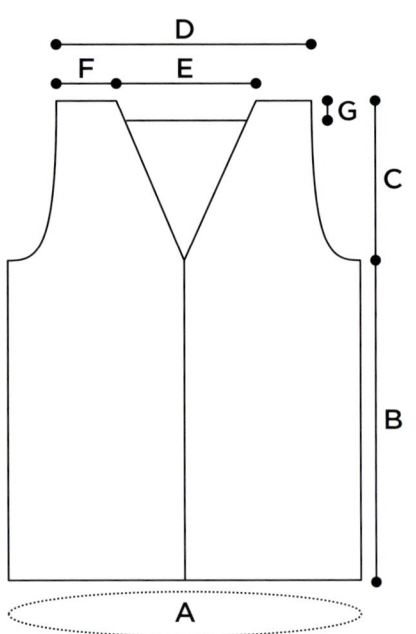

Double Moss Stitch, 4+1 sts

Double Moss Stitch, 4+3 sts

Diamond Pattern

- A 35.25 (38.25, 41.5, 44.5, 47.75, 50.75, 54)"
- B 16 (16, 16, 16, 16, 16.5, 17)"
- C 8 (8.5, 9, 9.5, 10, 10.5, 11)"
- D 12.75 (13, 13.5, 14, 15, 16.25, 17)"
- E 7 (7.25, 7.75, 8.25, 9, 9.5, 10)"
- F 3 (3, 3, 3, 3, 3.25, 3.5)"
- G 1"

DOUBLE CROSS PULLOVER

by Adrienne Larsen

FINISHED MEASUREMENTS
33 (36, 39, 42, 45, 48, 51, 54)" finished chest circumference; meant to be worn with 4" positive ease

YARN
Knit Picks Wool of the Andes™ (sport weight, 100% Peruvian Highland Wool; 137 yards/50g): Pampas Heather 25653, 11 (11, 13, 14, 15, 16, 18, 19) skeins

NEEDLES
US 4 (3.5mm) 16" and 32" circular needles and DPNs, or size to obtain gauge
US 3 (3.25mm) 16" circular needles, or one size smaller than size used to obtain gauge

NOTIONS
Yarn Needle
Stitch Markers
Cable Needle
Scrap Yarn or Stitch Holder

GAUGE
25 sts and 34 rows = 4" in Rib Pattern, blocked aggressively
32 sts and 34 rows = 4" in Cable Pattern, blocked aggressively

For pattern support, contact adrienne.larsen@gmail.com

Double Cross Pullover

Notes:
The classic styling of this pullover is updated with a modern cable design. The ribbed body flows seamlessly into parallel traveling cables.

This sweater is knit in the round, from the bottom up, and the neck edging is picked up and knit. The sleeves are worked separately, in the round, and then sewn to the body.

Charts are worked both flat and in the round. When working charts in the round, read each chart row from right to left as a RS row. When working charts flat, read RS rows (odd numbers) from right to left, and WS rows (even numbers) from left to right.

DIRECTIONS

Body

Rib Section
With larger needles, CO 209 (228, 247, 266, 285, 304, 323, 342) sts. Join to work in the rnd, being careful not to twist sts. PM for BOR.
Rnd 1: *(P2, K2) two times, P1, (K2, P2) two times, K2; rep from * to end.
Rep Rnd 1 until piece measures 10.5 (11.25, 10.75, 11.5, 11, 11.25, 11.25, 11.5)" from CO edge.

Cable Section
Note: For some Body chart rows, the cables cross over BOR and appear to shift BOR. Do not shift BOR M—it will be in the middle of the cable sts.
Setup Rnd 1: Work Setup Rnd 1 of Body chart to end.
253 (276, 299, 322, 345, 368, 391, 414) sts.
Setup Rnd 2: Work Setup Rnd 2 of Body chart to end.
Setup Rnd 3: Work Setup Rnd 3 of Body chart to end.
264 (288, 312, 336, 360, 384, 408, 432) sts.
Rnds 1-20: Work next rnd of Body chart to end.
Work Rnds 1-20 1 (0, 1, 1, 1, 1, 1, 1) more time(s).
Work Rnds 1 through 3 (19, 15, 1 only, 7, 7, 9, 9) one more time.

Separate for Underarm
Next Rnd: Work 123 (123, 135, 159, 159, 185, 171, 171) Front sts in pattern, BO 28 (40, 28, 40, 52, 40, 52, 64) sts, work 104 (104, 128, 128, 128, 152, 152, 152) Back sts in pattern, BO 28 (40, 28, 40, 52, 40, 52, 64) sts, removing BOR M as you come to it. 104 (104, 128, 128, 128, 152, 152, 152) Front sts; 104 (128, 128, 128, 128, 152, 152, 152) Back sts.
Place Back sts on holder and begin working the Front flat.

Front
Row 1 (RS): Work Row 5 (1, 17, 3, 9, 9, 11, 11) of Shoulder chart.
Row 2 (WS): Work next row of Shoulder chart.
Row 3: Work next row of Shoulder chart.
Rep Rows 2-3 through Row 20 of Shoulder chart.
Work Rows 1-20 of Shoulder chart 0 (0, 1, 1, 0, 0, 1, 1) more time(s).
Work Rows 1 through 13 (13, 3, 3, 13, 13, 3, 3) of Shoulder chart.

Next Row (WS): Work 52 (52, 64, 64, 64, 76, 76, 76) sts in pattern as established, and place on holders for Right Front, work 52 (52, 64, 64, 64, 76, 76, 76) sts.

Left Front
Row 1 (RS): Work Left Front chart.
Row 2 (WS): Work Left Front Chart.
Cont in pattern to end of Left Front chart. Place remaining 20 (20, 32, 32, 32, 44, 44, 44) sts on holder. Break yarn.

Right Front
Place Right Front sts on needles. Attach yarn to RS.
Row 1 (RS): Work Right Front chart Row 1.
Row 2 (WS): Work next row of Right Front chart.
Cont in pattern to end of Right Front chart. Place remaining 20 (20, 32, 32, 32, 44, 44, 44) sts on holder. Break yarn.

Back
Place Back sts on needles. Attach yarn to RS.
Row 1 (RS): Work Row 5 (1, 7, 3, 9, 9, 11, 11) of Shoulder chart.
Row 2 (WS): Work next row of Shoulder chart.
Row 3: Work next row of Shoulder chart.
Rep Rows 2-3 through Row 20 of Shoulder chart.
Work Rows 1-20 of Shoulder chart 1 (1, 2, 2, 2, 2, 3, 3) more time(s).
Work Rows 1 through 19 (19, 9, 9, 19, 19, 9, 9) of Shoulder chart.

Attach Fronts to Back
Turn sweater inside out so RSs are tog and line up Front and Back to prepare for seaming.
Seam 20 (20, 32, 32, 32, 44, 44, 44) sts from Left Front to Back using 3-Needle Bind Off, work 64 sts in pattern, seam 20 (20, 32, 32, 32, 44, 44, 44) sts from Right Front to Back using 3-Needle Bind Off.

Neck Edging
Place Back Neck sts on smaller needles and attach yarn with RS facing.

Sizes 33", 36", 39", 45" & 51" Only
Setup Rnd: Work Back Neck Chart A (54 sts), PM, PU and K 11 sts along straight section of left neck edge, PM, PU and K 32 sts along left diagonal edge, PM, PU and K 32 sts along right diagonal edge, PU and K 11 sts along straight section of right neck edge, PM for BOR. 140 sts.
Rnd 1: Remove M, Sl1, PM for BOR, (P1, K2, P1) to 1 st before M, PM (there are now 52 sts for Back Neck), P1, remove M, (K2, P2) to last 3 sts, K2, P1.
Rnd 2: K2tog, work in pattern as established to 2 sts before next M, SSK, SM, K2tog, work to next M, SM, (K2tog, work to 2 sts before next M, SSK, SM) two times, work in pattern to 2 sts before next M, SSK. 8 sts dec.
Rnd 3, and all odd-numbered rnds: Work in pattern.
Rnd 4: Rep Rnd 2.

Rnd 6: P2tog, work in pattern to 2 sts before next M, SSP, SM, P2tog, work to next M, SM, (P2tog, work to 2 sts before next M, SSP, SM) two times, work in pattern to 2 sts before next M, SSP. 8 sts dec.
Rnd 8: Rep Rnd 6.
BO in pattern.

Sizes 42", 48" & 54" Only
Setup Rnd: Work Back Neck Chart B (52 sts), PM, PU and K 12 sts along straight section of left neck edge, PM, PU and K 32 sts along left diagonal edge, PM, PU and K 32 sts along right diagonal edge, PU and K 12 sts along straight section of right neck edge, PM for BOR. 140 sts.
Rnd 1: (K1, P2, K1) to end.
Rnd 2: P2tog, work in pattern as established to 2 sts before next M, SSP, SM, P2tog, work to next M, SM, (P2tog, work to 2 sts before next M, SSP, SM) two times, work in pattern to 2 sts before next M, SSP. 8 sts dec.
Rnd 3, and all odd-numbered rnds: Work in pattern to end.
Rnd 4: Rep Rnd 2.
Rnd 6: K2tog, work in pattern to 2 sts before next M, SSK, SM, K2tog, work to next M, SM, (K2tog, work to 2 sts before next M, SSK, SM) two times, work in pattern to 2 sts before next M, SSK. 8 sts dec.
Rnd 8: Rep Rnd 6.
BO in pattern.

Sleeves (make two the same)
With larger needles, CO 50 (50, 50, 54, 54, 54, 60, 60) sts. Join to work in the rnd, being careful not to twist sts. PM for BOR.

Sizes 33", 36" & 39" Only
Rnd 1: P1, (K2, P2) three times, K2, P1, (K2, P2) four times, K2, P1, (K2, P2) three times, K2, P1.

Sizes 42", 45" & 48" Only
Rnd 1: K1, (P2, K2) four times, P1, (K2, P2) four times, K2, P1, (K2, P2) four times, K1.

Sizes 51" & 54" Only
Rnd 1: K1, *P1, (K2, P2) four times, K2; rep from * two more times, P1, K1.

All Sizes
Cont in pattern until piece measures 17 (17, 17, 17.5, 17.5, 18, 18, 18)" while AT THE SAME TIME increasing 1 st each side every 9 (8, 7, 7, 5, 5, 4, 4) rnds 15 (17, 16, 12, 8, 14, 1, 11) times, then every 0 (0, 8, 8, 6, 6, 5, 5) rnds 0 (0, 3, 7, 17, 13, 29, 21) times, working new sts into pattern and ending 14 (20, 14, 20, 26, 20, 26, 32) sts before end of last rnd. 80 (84, 88, 92, 104, 108, 120, 124) sts.

Shape Sleeve Cap
Sleeve cap is worked flat.

A 33 (36, 39, 42, 45, 48, 51, 54)"
B 16 (16.25, 16.5, 16.75, 17, 17.5, 17.5, 17.75)"
C 6.5 (7, 7.5, 8, 8.5, 8.5, 9.5, 9.5)"
D 5.25"
E 13 (13, 16, 16, 16, 19, 19, 19)"
F 8"
G 8 (8, 8, 8.75, 8.75, 8.75, 9.5, 9.5)"
H 17 (17, 17, 17.5, 17.5, 18, 18, 18)"
I 5.5 (6, 6.5, 7, 7.5, 7.5, 8.5, 8.5)"
J 12.75 (13.5, 14, 14.75, 16.75, 17.25, 19.25, 19.75)"

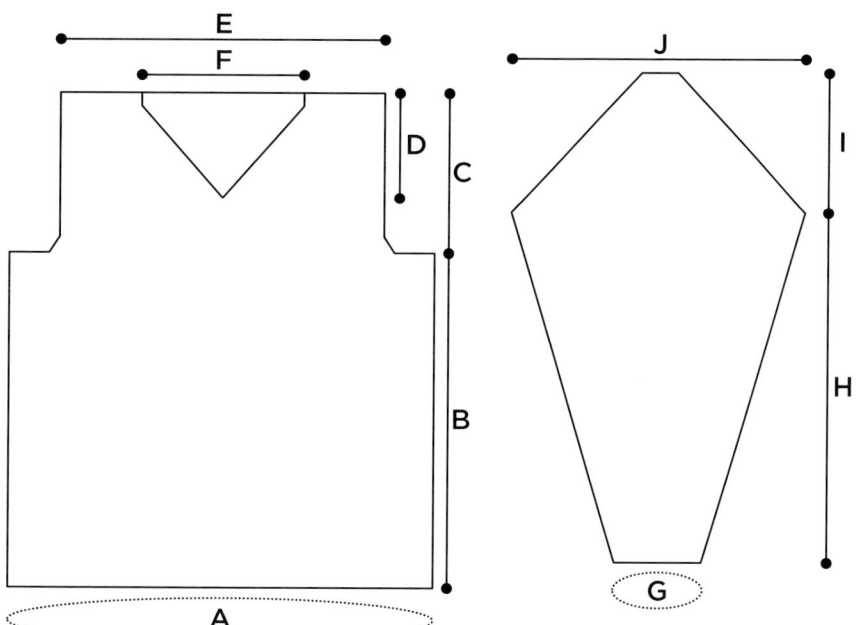

Row 1 (RS): BO 28 (40, 28, 40, 52, 40, 52, 64) sts, work in pattern to end. 52 (44, 60, 52, 52, 68, 68, 60) sts.
Row 2 (WS): Work in pattern to end.
Dec Row: P1, K2tog, work in pattern to last 3 sts, SSK, P1. 2 sts dec.

Cont in pattern while working Dec Row every other row 5 (1, 5, 1, 0, 6, 4, 1) time(s), then every four rows 6 (11, 8, 13, 15, 9, 13, 16) times, then every other row 5 (2, 6, 2, 1, 7, 5, 2) times. 18 (14, 20, 18, 18, 22, 22, 20) sts.
BO 6 (5, 7, 6, 6, 7, 7, 7) sts in pattern at beginning of next two rows. BO remaining 6 (4, 6, 6, 6, 8, 8, 6) sts in pattern.

Finishing

Sew in sleeves. Weave in ends, wash, and block aggressively to diagram measurements.

LEGEND

No Stitch
Placeholder—no stitch made

K
RS: Knit stitch
WS: Purl stitch

P
RS: Purl stitch
WS: Knit stitch

M1P
Make 1 purl stitch

P2tog
RS: Purl 2 stitches together as one stitch
WS: Knit 2 stitches together as one stitch

SSP
RS: (Slip 1 knit-wise) twice; slip the 2 stitches back to left-hand needle and purl them together through the back loops
WS: work SSK—(Slip 1 knit-wise) twice; insert left-hand needle into front of these 2 stitches and knit them together

SSSP
RS: (Slip 1 knit-wise) three times; slip the 3 stitches back to left-hand needle and purl them together through the back loops
WS: work SSSK—(Slip 1 knit-wise) three times; insert left-hand needle from the front to the back of all stitches at the same time and knit them together

P3tog
RS: Purl 3 stitches together as one
WS: Knit 3 stitches together as one

Cable 2 Over 2 Right, Purl back (2/2 RPC)
Sl2 to CN, hold in back; K2, P2 from CN

Cable 2 Over 2 Left, Purl back (2/2 LPC)
Sl2 to CN, hold in front; P2, K2 from CN

Cable 2 Over 2 Right (2/2 RC)
Sl2 to CN, hold in back; K2, K2 from CN

Cable 2 Over 2 Left (2/2 LC)
Sl2 to CN, hold in front; K2, K2 from CN

Cable 2 Over 2 Right, Knit 2 center back (2/2/2 RC)
Sl4 to CN, hold in back; K2, Sl 2 leftmost sts from CN to left hand needle, move CN to front, K2 from left hand needle, K2 from CN

Cable 2 Over 4 Left, Purl back (2/4 LPC)
Sl2 to CN, hold in front; P4, K2 from CN

Cable 2 Over 4 Right, Purl back (2/4 RPC)
Sl4 to CN, hold in back; K2, P4 from CN

Pattern Repeat

Back Neck—Chart A

Back Neck—Chart B

Body

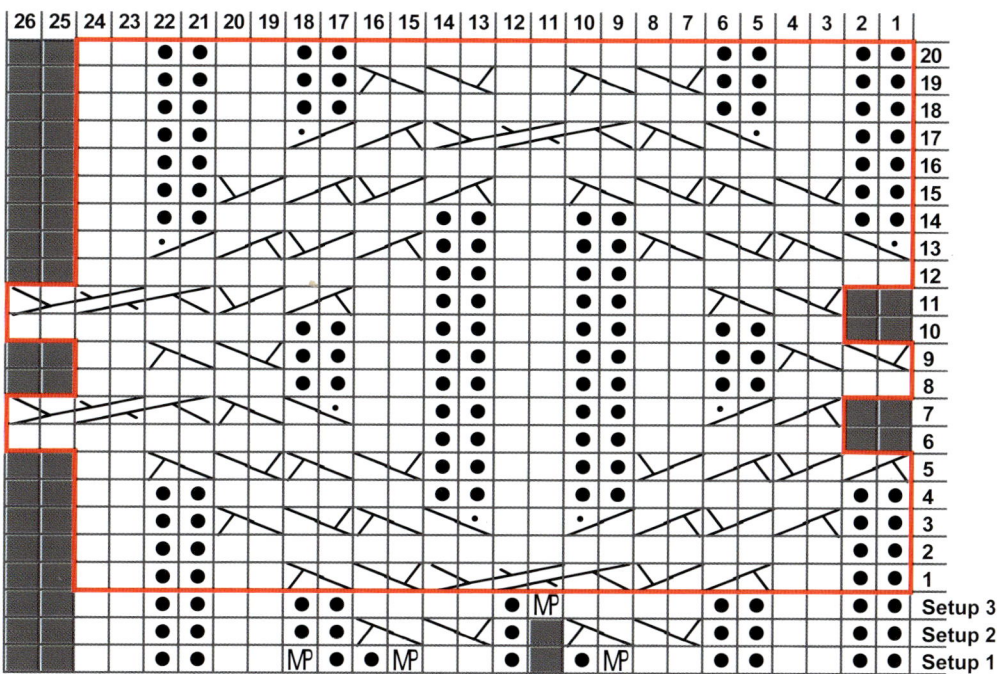

Shoulder

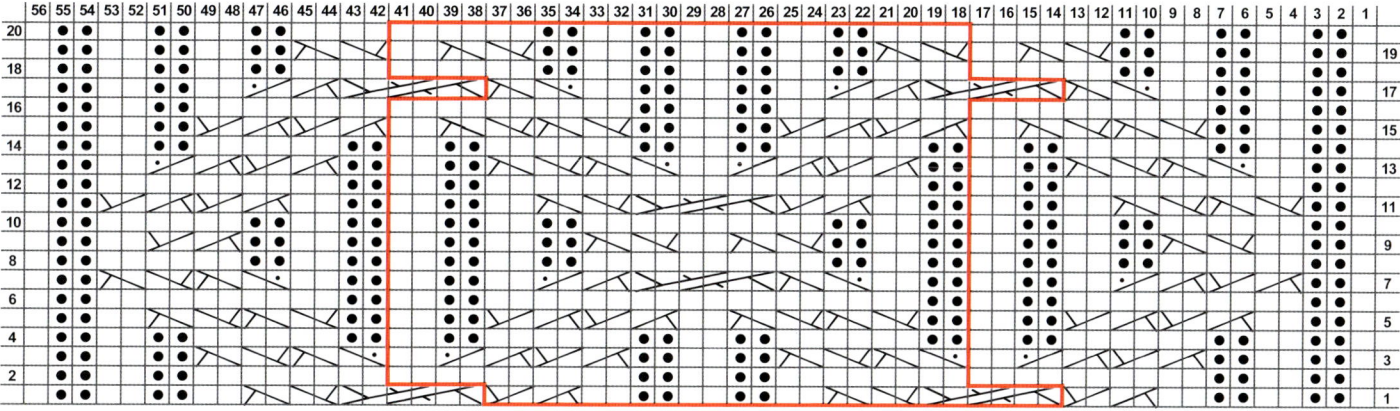

Right Front—Sizes 33" & 36"

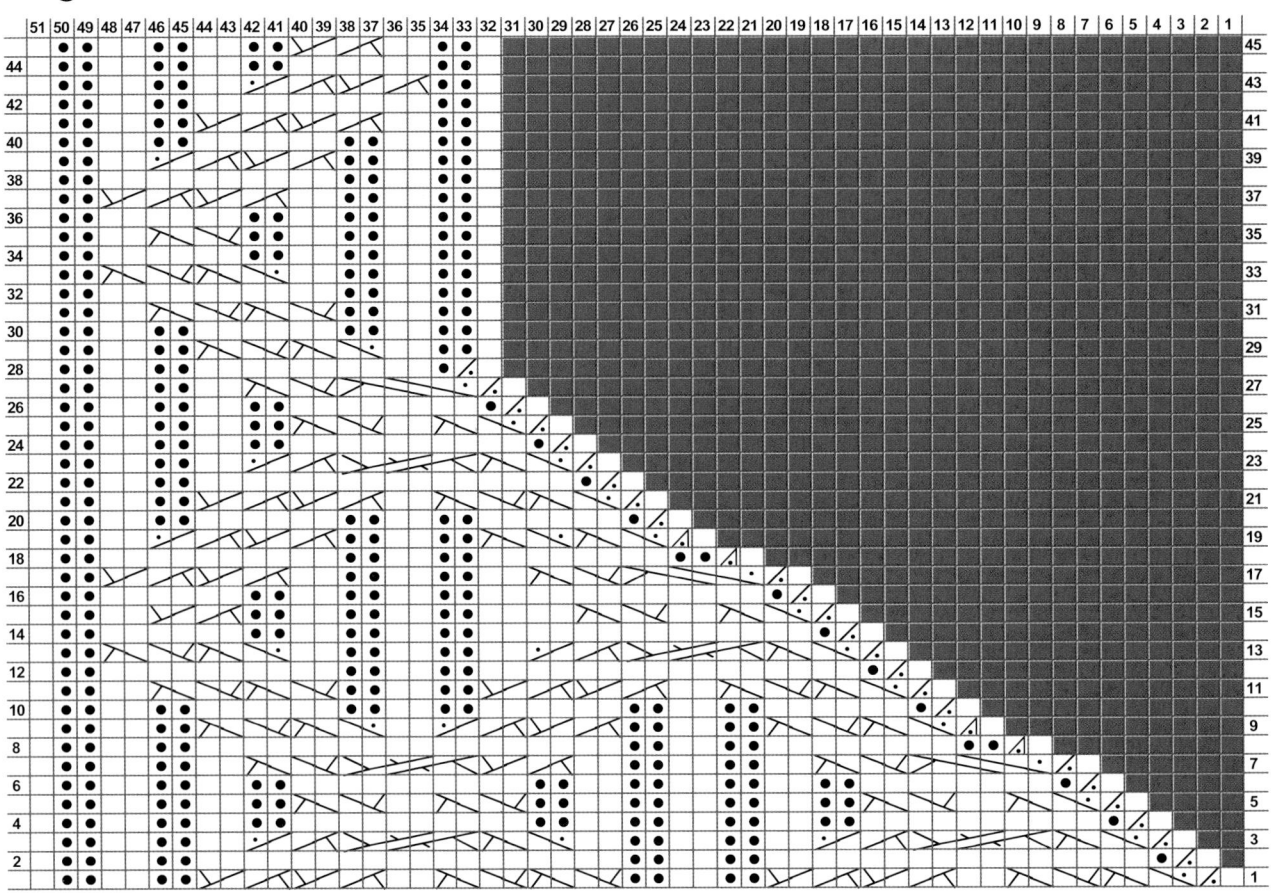

Left Front—Sizes 33" & 36"

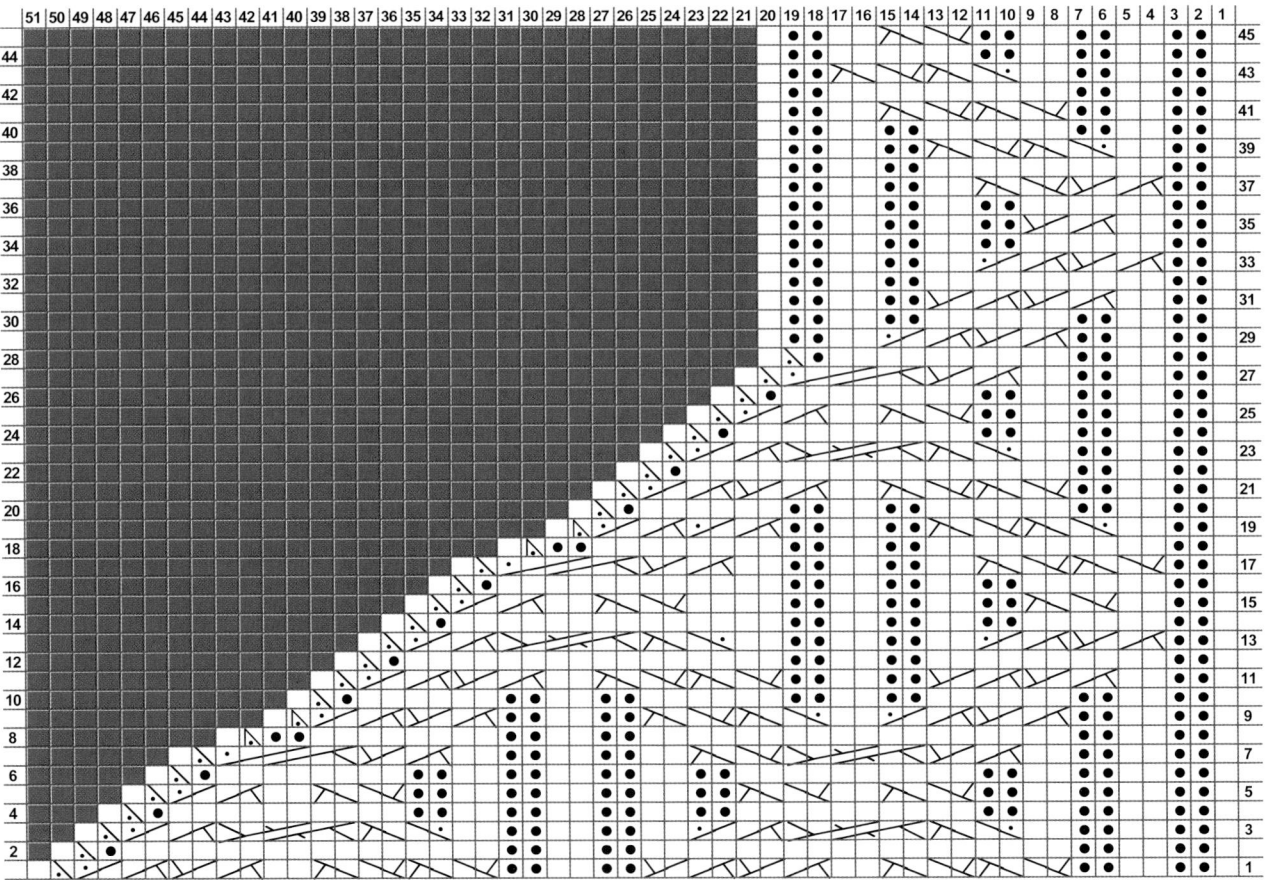

Right Front—Sizes 39", 42" & 45"

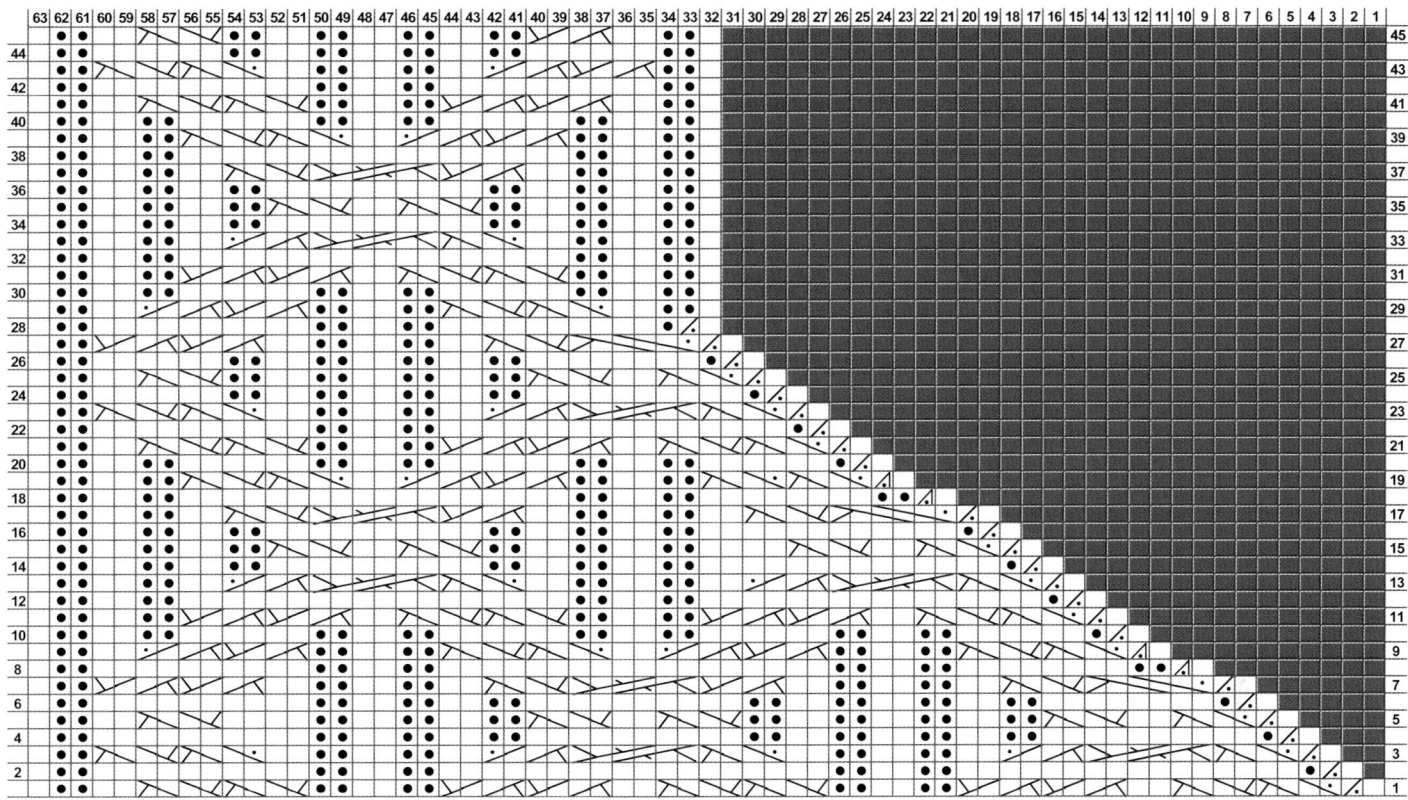

Left Front—Sizes 39", 42" & 45"

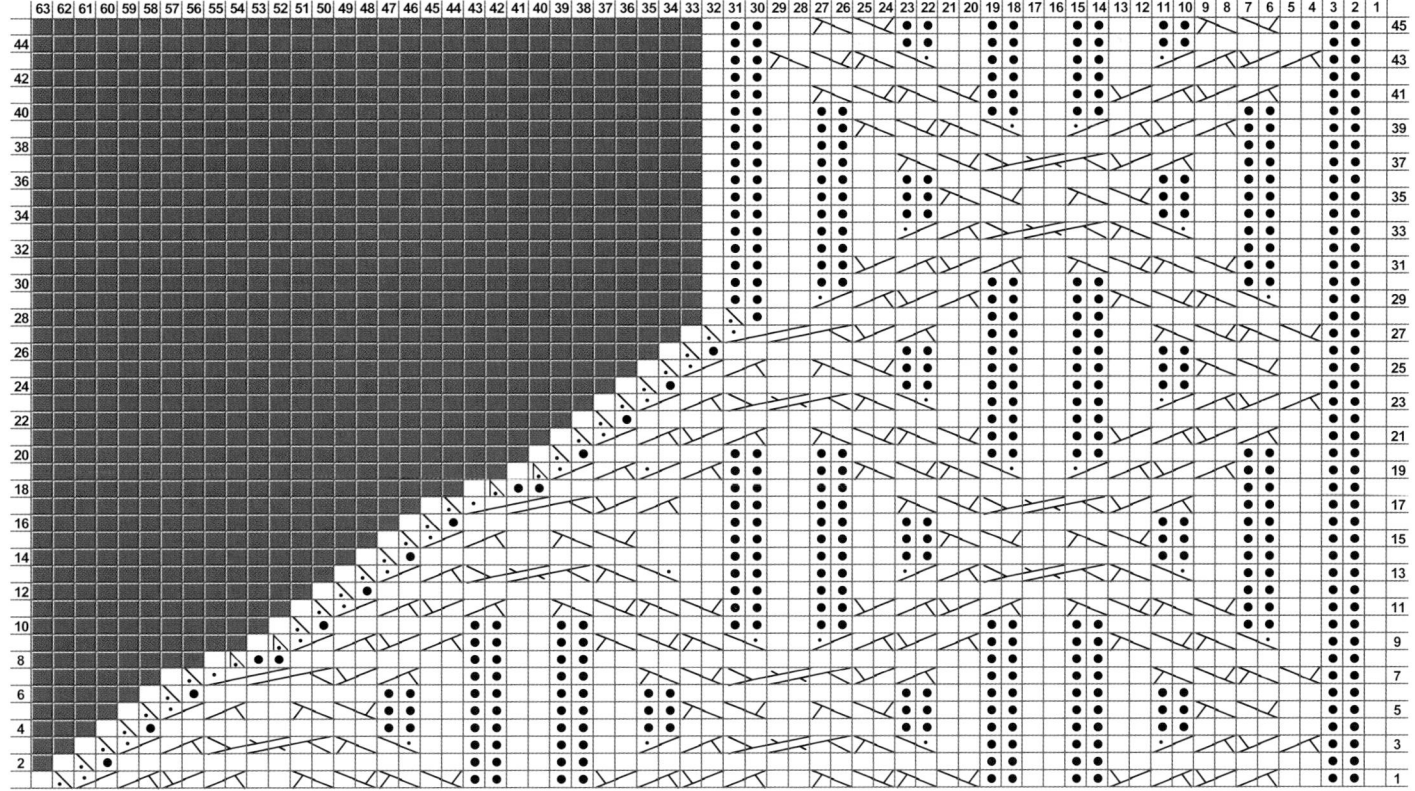

Double Cross Pullover

Right Front—Sizes 48", 51" & 54"

Left Front—Sizes 48", 51" & 54"

Double Cross Pullover 33

EMPIRE

by Kirsten Joel

FINISHED MEASUREMENTS
32.25 (36.25, 40.25, 44.25, 48.25, 52.25)" finished chest circumference; meant to be worn with 3-4" positive ease

YARN
Knit Picks Wool of the Andes™ (sport weight, 100% Peruvian Highland Wool; 137 yards/50g): Forest Heather 25285, 11 (13, 14, 16, 17, 19) skeins

NEEDLES
US 3 (3.5mm) straight or circular needles (24" or longer), or size to obtain gauge
US 3 (3.5mm) DPNs or 16" circular needles, or size to obtain gauge

NOTIONS
Yarn Needle
Stitch Markers
Scrap Yarn or Stitch Holder

GAUGE
24 sts and 38 rows = 4" in Stockinette Stitch, blocked

For pattern support, contact kirstenfjoel@kleverknitsdesigns.com

Empire

Notes:
Empire is a modern interpretation of a traditional gansey sweater, with set-in sleeves updating the traditionally boxy gansey sweater for a modern fit. Both yoke and sleeves are textured with a high relief pattern that calls to mind sleek architectural lines, giving it its name, Empire.

The sweater is knit in pieces, flat, and then seamed together. The neckband is then picked up and added at the end.

1x1 Rib (flat over a multiple of 2 sts plus 1)
Row 1: K1 (K1, P1) to last 2 sts, K2.
Row 2: K1 (P1, K1) to last 2 sts, P1, K1.
Rep Rows 1-2 for pattern.

Textured Stitch Pattern (flat over a multiple of 3 sts)
Row 1 (RS): K across.
Row 2 (WS): K1, P to last st, K1.
Row 3: K1 (K1, P2) to last 2 sts, K2.
Row 4: K1, P1, (K2, P1) to last st, K1.
Rep Rows 1-4 for pattern.

DIRECTIONS

Back
CO 99 (111, 123, 135, 147, 159) sts.
Work 1x1 Rib until piece measures 2.5" from CO edge.
Work St st until piece measures 10.5 (10.5, 10.75, 10.75, 11, 11.25)" from CO edge.
Work Textured Stitch Pattern until piece measures 15.75 (15.75, 16.25, 16.25, 16.75, 16.75)" from CO edge, ending with a WS row. Note final row worked of Textured Stitch Pattern.

Armhole Shaping
BO 4 (5, 6, 8, 9, 10) sts at beginning of next two rows. 91 (101, 111, 119, 129, 139) sts.

Sizes 44.25", 48.25" & 52.25"
BO - (-, -, 2, 2, 2) sts at beginning of next two rows. 91 (101, 111, 115, 125, 135) sts.

All Sizes Resume
Armhole Dec Row (RS): K2, K2tog, work in pattern to last 4 sts, SSK, K2. 2 sts dec.
Rep Armhole Dec Row every RS row 3 (4, 6, 6, 8, 9) more times, then every fourth row 1 (2, 2, 2, 2, 2) more times. 81 (87, 93, 103, 111) sts
Work even in pattern until armhole measures 6.5 (7, 7.5, 8, 8.5, 9)" from armhole bind off, ending with a WS row.

Neck Shaping
Setup Row (RS): Work 22 (24, 26, 27, 29, 32) sts in pattern, join second ball of yarn and BO center 37 (39, 41, 43, 45, 47) sts, work to end. 22 (24, 26, 27, 29, 32) sts for each shoulder. Work both shoulders at once.
Row 1 (WS): Work even in pattern.
Row 2 (RS): Work in pattern to last 4 sts of right shoulder, SSK, K2; with second ball of yarn, K2, K2tog, work to end of left shoulder.
Row 3: Work even in pattern.
Rep Rows 2-3 once more. 20 (22, 24, 25, 27, 30) sts.
BO all sts.

Front
CO 99 (111, 123, 135, 147, 159) sts.
Work 1x1 Rib until piece measures 2.5" from CO edge.
Work St st until piece measures 10.5 (10.5, 10.75, 10.75, 11, 11.25)" from CO edge.
Work Textured Stitch Pattern until piece measures 15.75 (15.75, 16.25, 16.25, 16.75, 16.75)" from CO edge, ending with the same row of Textured Stitch Pattern as on Back.

Armhole Shaping
BO 4 (5, 6, 8, 9, 10) sts at beginning of next two rows. 91 (101, 111, 119, 129, 139) sts.

Sizes 44.25", 48.25" & 52.25"
BO - (-, -, 2, 2, 2) sts at beginning of next two rows. 91 (101, 111, 115, 125, 135) sts.

All Sizes Resume
Armhole Dec Row (RS): K2, K2tog, work in pattern to last 4 sts, SSK, K2. 2 sts dec.
Rep Armhole Dec Row every RS row 3 (4, 6, 6, 8, 9) more times, then every fourth row 1 (2, 2, 2, 2, 2) more times. 81 (87, 93, 103, 111) sts
Work even until armhole measures 3.75 (4.25, 4.75, 5.25, 5.5, 6)" from armhole bind off, ending with a WS row.

Neck Shaping
Setup Row (RS): Work 36 (39, 41, 43, 45, 49) sts in pattern, join second ball of yarn and BO center 9 (9, 11, 11, 13, 13) sts, work to end. 36 (39, 41, 43, 45, 49) sts for each side.
Row 1 (WS): Work in pattern to neck edge; with second ball of yarn BO 3 sts, work to end.
Row 2 (RS): Work in pattern to neck edge; with second ball of yarn BO 3 sts, work to end. 33 (36, 38, 40, 42, 46) sts. Continuing as established, BO 2 sts from each neck edge five more times, then BO 1 st from neck edge 3 (4, 4, 5, 5, 6) times. 20 (22, 24, 25, 27, 30) sts remain on each side.
Work even in pattern until armhole measures 7 (7.5, 8, 8.5, 9, 9.5)" from armhole bind off.
BO all sts.

Sleeves (make two the same)
CO 51 (53, 55, 61, 63, 65) sts.
Work 1x1 Rib until piece measures 2.5" from CO edge.
Switch to working St st.
Inc Row (RS): K2, M1, work to last 2 sts, M1, K2. 2 sts inc.
Work even for 11 (9, 9, 7, 7, 5, 5) rows.

Rep these 12 (10, 8, 8, 6, 6) rows 10 (13, 16, 17, 20, 23) more times. 73 (81, 89, 97, 105, 113) sts.

AT THE SAME TIME, when piece measures 15.5 (15.25, 15.25, 15, 15, 14)" from CO edge, begin working in Textured Stitch Pattern.

Work even until piece measures 19 (19, 19.25, 19.25, 19.5, 19.75)" from CO edge, ending with the same row of Textured Stitch Pattern as Front and Back.

Cap Shaping

BO 4 (5, 6, 8, 9, 10) sts at beginning of next two rows. 65 (71, 75, 81, 85, 93) sts.

Sizes 44.25", 48.25" & 52.25"

BO - (-, -, 2, 2, 2) sts at beginning of next two rows. 65 (71, 75, 75, 81, 89) sts.

All Sizes Resume

Double Dec Row (RS): K2, K2tog twice, work in pattern to last 6 sts, SSK twice, K2. 4 sts dec.

Rep Double Dec Row every RS row 2 (3, 3, 3, 3, 4) more times. 53 (55, 61, 61, 67, 69) sts.

Dec Row (RS): K2, K2tog, work to last 4 sts, SSK, K2. 2 sts dec.

Rep Dec Row every RS row 8 (9, 10, 10, 11, 12) more times, then every fourth row two more times, then every RS row 2 (2, 3, 3, 4, 4) more times. 27 (27, 29, 29, 31, 31) sts.

BO 4 sts at beginning of next two rows. 19 (19, 21, 21, 23, 23) sts.

BO all remaining sts.

Finishing

Weave in ends, wash, and block to diagram.
Sew shoulder seams. Sew sleeves to body. Sew underarm and side seams.

Neckband

Note: PU st counts are approximate; since neckband is worked in St st, just be sure to pick up sts neatly.

With RS facing, and beginning at right shoulder seam, PU and K 41 (43, 45, 47, 49, 51) sts along back neck edge and 61 (67, 71, 75, 81, 85) sts along front neck edge. PM for BOR and join for working in the rnd. 102 (110, 116, 122, 130, 136) sts.

Knit six rnds.

BO all sts.

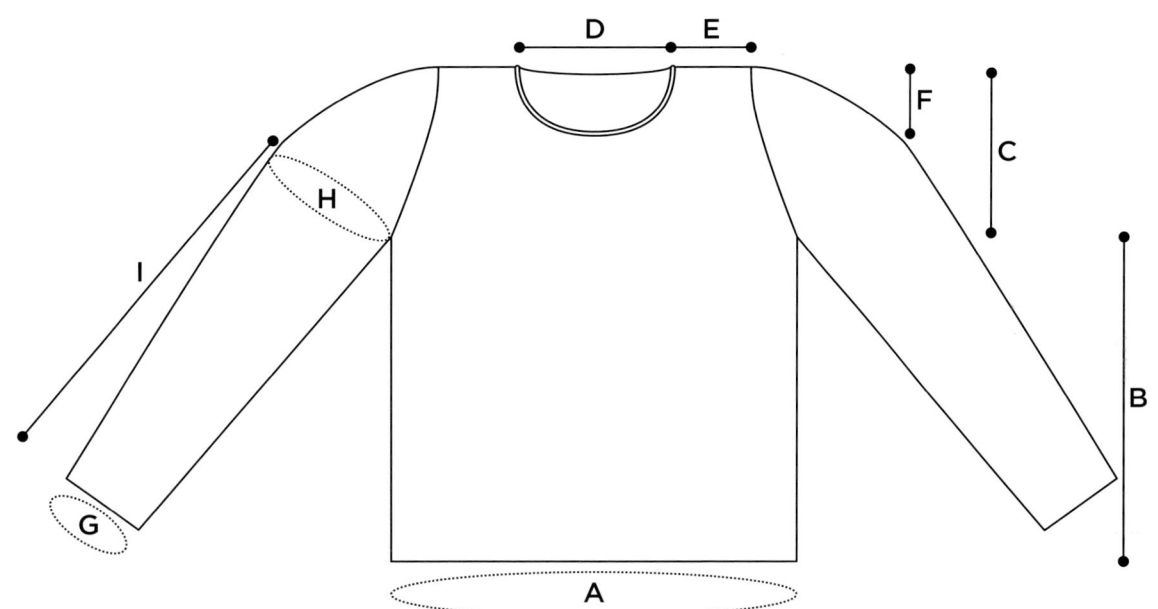

- A 32.25 (36.25, 40.25, 44.25, 48.25, 52.25)"
- B 15.75 (15.75, 16.25, 16.25, 16.75, 16.75)"
- C 7 (7.5, 8, 8.5, 9, 9.5)"
- D 7 (7.25, 7.5, 8, 8.25, 8.5)"
- E 3.25 (3.75, 4, 4.25, 4.5, 5)"
- F 3.25 (3.25, 3.25, 3.25, 3.5, 3.5)"
- G 8.5 (8.75, 9.25, 10.25, 10.5, 10.75)"
- H 12 (13.25, 14.75, 16, 17.25, 18.75)"
- I 19 (19, 19.25, 19.25, 19.5, 19.75)"

Empire

GRAY DAYS

by Hope Vickman

FINISHED MEASUREMENTS
34.5 (38.75, 42.25, 46.25, 51.25)" finished chest circumference; meant to be worn with 1-3" positive ease

YARN
Knit Picks Wool of the Andes™ (worsted weight, 100% Peruvian Highland Wool; 110 yards/50g): Icicle Heather 25992, 12 (14, 16, 17, 19) skeins

NEEDLES
US 4 (3.5mm) 16" and 32" circular needles, or size to obtain gauge
US 4 (3.5mm) DPNs or two 24" circular needles for two circulars technique or 32" or longer circular needles for Magic Loop technique, or size to obtain gauge

NOTIONS
Yarn Needle
16 Stitch Markers
2 Removable Stitch Markers
Cable Needle
Scrap Yarn or 3 Stitch Holders

GAUGE
22 sts and 30 rnds = 4" in Stockinette Stitch in the round, blocked
28 sts and 30 rows = 4" in Center Cable Pattern, blocked
30 sts and 30 rows = 4" in Open Cable Pattern, blocked

For pattern support, contact hopehafs@hotmail.com

Gray Days

Notes:

Gansey-style sweaters similar to this one have been worn by fisherfolk for hundreds of years. Densely knit and uniquely patterned, this sweater calls to mind images of the fishing line unspooling and the waves lapping on a gray and dreary day.

This unisex sweater is knit in the round from the bottom up. Sleeve stitches are picked up around the armholes and worked in the round from the shoulder down. Please note that the Center Cable pattern is wider for the larger sizes; be sure to follow the correct set of Center Cable instructions for the size you are knitting.

Stitch patterns are written and charted. Charts are worked both flat and in the round. When working charts in the round, read each chart row from right to left as a RS row. When working charts flat, read RS rows (even numbers) from right to left, and WS rows (odd numbers) from left to right. All flat stitch patterns begin with a WS Row 1.

Reverse Stockinette Stitch (Rev St st, flat over any number of sts)
Row 1 (WS): K across.
Row 2 (RS): P across.
Rep Rows 1-2 for pattern.

Reverse Stockinette Stitch (Rev St st, in the round over any number of sts)
All Rnds: P all.

Cable 2 over 2 Left (2/2 LC)
Sl2 to CN, hold in front; K2, K2 from CN.

Cable 2 over 2 Right (2/2 RC)
Sl2 to CN, hold in back; K2, K2 from CN.

Cable 2 Over 2 Left, Purl back (2/2 LPC)
Sl2 to CN, hold in front; P2, K2 from CN.

Cable 2 Over 2 Right, Purl back (2/2 RPC)
Sl2 to CN, hold in back; K2, P2 from CN.

Cable 2 Over 1 Left, Purl back (2/1 LPC)
Sl2 to CN, hold in front; P1, K2 from CN.

Cable 2 Over 1 Right, Purl back (2/1 RPC)
Sl1 to CN, hold in back; K2, P1 from CN.

Welts (flat over 6 sts)
Row 1 (WS): P1, K4, P1.
Row 2 (RS): Sl1 WYIB, P4, Sl1 WYIB.
Row 3: P6.
Row 4: Sl1 WYIB, K4, Sl1 WYIB.

Welts (in the round over 6 sts)
Rnd 1: K1, P4, K1.
Rnd 2: Sl1 WYIB, P4, Sl1 WYIB.
Rnd 3: K6.
Rnd 4: Sl1 WYIB, K4, Sl1 WYIB.

Open Cable (flat over 14 sts)
Row 1 (WS): K5, P4, K5.
Row 2 (RS): P5, 2/2 LC, P5.
Row 3: Rep Row 1.
Row 4: P3, 2/2 RPC, 2/2 LPC, P3.
Row 5: K3, P2, K4, P2, K3.
Row 6: P2, 2/1 RPC, P4, 2/1 LPC, P2.
Row 7: K2, P2, K6, P2, K2.
Row 8: P2, K2, P6, K2, P2.
Row 9: Rep Row 7.
Row 10: Rep Row 8.
Row 11: Rep Row 7.
Row 12: P2, 2/1 LPC, P4, 2/1 RPC, P2.
Row 13: Rep Row 5.
Row 14: P3, 2/2 LPC, 2/2 RPC, P3.

Open Cable (in the round over 14 sts)
Rnd 1: P5, K4, P5.
Rnd 2: P5, 2/2 LC, P5.
Rnd 3: Rep Rnd 1.
Rnd 4: P3, 2/2 RPC, 2/2 LPC, P3.
Rnd 5: P3, K2, P4, K2, P3.
Rnd 6: P2, 2/1 RPC, P4, 2/1 LPC, P2.
Rnd 7: P2, K2, P6, K2, P2.
Rnds 8-11: Rep Rnd 7 four more times.
Rnd 12: P2, 2/1 LPC, P4, 2/1 RPC, P2.
Rnd 13: Rep Rnd 5.
Rnd 14: P3, 2/2 LPC, 2/2 RPC, P3.

Center Cable—Size 34.5" (flat over 30 sts)
Row 1 (WS): K2, P2, K6, P2, K2, (P2, K6) two times.
Row 2 (RS): P4, 2/2 RPC, P4, 2/2 RC, P2, 2/2 LPC, P5, K1, P2.
Row 3: K8, P2, K4, P4, K6, P2, K4.
Row 4: P2, 2/2 RPC, P4, 2/2 RPC, K2, P4, 2/2 LPC, P6.
Row 5: (K6, P2) two times, K2, P2, K6, P2, K2.
Row 6: P2, K1, P5, 2/2 RPC, P2, 2/2 LC, P4, 2/2 LPC, P4.
Row 7: K4, P2, K6, P4, K4, P2, K8.
Row 8: P6, 2/2 RPC, P4, K2, 2/2 LPC, P4, 2/2 LPC, P2.

Center Cable—Size 34.5" (in the round over 30 sts)
Rnd 1: (P6, K2) two times, P2, K2, P6, K2, P2.
Rnd 2: P4, 2/2 RPC, P4, 2/2 RC, P2, 2/2 LPC, p5, K1, P2.
Rnd 3: P4, K2, P6, K4, P4, K2, P8.
Rnd 4: P2, 2/2 RPC, P4, 2/2 RPC, K2, P4, 2/2 LPC, P6.
Rnd 5: P2, K2, P6, K2, P2, (K2, P6) two times.
Rnd 6: P2, K1, P5, 2/2 RPC, P2, 2/2 LC, P4, 2/2 LPC, P4.
Rnd 7: P8, K2, P4, K4, P6, K2, P4.
Rnd 8: P6, 2/2 RPC, P4, K2, 2/2 LPC, P4, 2/2 LPC, P2.

Center Cable—Size 38.75" (flat over 42 sts)
Row 1 (WS): K2, (K6, P2) two times, K2, P2, (K6, P2) two times, K4.
Row 2 (RS): P2, (2/2 RPC, P4) two times, 2/2 RC, P2, (2/2 LPC, P4) two times, P2.
Row 3: (K6, P2) two times, K4, P4, (K6, P2) two times, K2.
Row 4: P2, K1, P1, (P4, 2/2 RPC) two times, K2, (P4, 2/2 LPC) two times, P4.
Row 5: K4, (P2, K6) two times, P2, K2, (P2, K6) two times, K2.
Row 6: P2, (P4, 2/2 RPC) two times, P2, 2/2 LC, (P4, 2/2 LPC) two times, P2.
Row 7: K2, (P2, K6) two times, P4, K4, (P2, K6) two times.
Row 8: (P4, 2/2 RPC) two times, P4, K2, (2/2 LPC, P4) two times, P1, K1, P2.

Center Cable—Size 38.75" (in the round over 42 sts)
Rnd 1: P4, (K2, P6) two times, K2, P2, (K2, P6) two times, P2.
Rnd 2: P2, (2/2 RPC, P4) two times, 2/2 RC, P2, (2/2 LPC, P4) two times, P2.
Rnd 3: P2, (K2, P6) two times, K4, P4, (K2, P6) two times.
Rnd 4: P2, K1, P1, (P4, 2/2 RPC) two times, K2, (P4, 2/2 LPC) two times, P4.
Rnd 5: P2, (P6, K2) two times, P2, (K2, P6) two times, K2, P4.
Rnd 6: P2, (P4, 2/2 RPC) two times, P2, 2/2 LC, (P4, 2/2 LPC) two times, P2.
Rnd 7: (P6, K2) two times, P4, K4, (P6, K2) two times, P2.
Rnd 8: (P4, 2/2 RPC) two times, P4, K2, (2/2 LPC, P4) two times, P1, K1, P2.

Center Cable—Size 42.25" (flat over 54 sts)
Row 1 (WS): (K6, P2), three times, K2, (P2, K6) three times, P2, K2.
Row 2 (RS): P2, K1, P5, (2/2 RPC, P4) two times, 2/2 RC, P2, (2/2 LPC, P4) three times.
Row 3: K4, (P2, K6) two times, P2, K4, P4, (K6, P2) two times, K8.
Row 4: P2, (P4, 2/2 RPC) three times, K2, (P4, 2/2 LPC) three times, P2.
Row 5: K2, (P2, K6) three times, P2, K2, (P2, K6) three times.
Row 6: (P4, 2/2 RPC) three times, P2, 2/2 LC, (P4, 2/2 LPC) two times, P5, K1, P2.
Row 7: K8, (P2, K6) two times, P4, K4, (P2, K6) two times, P2, K4.
Row 8: P2, (2/2 RPC, P4) three times, K2, (2/2 LPC, P4) three times, P2.

Center Cable—Size 42.25" (in the round over 54 sts)
Rnd 1: P2, (K2, P6) three times, K2, P2, (K2, P6) three times.
Rnd 2: P2, K1, P5, (2/2 RPC, P4) two times, 2/2 RC, P2, (2/2 LPC, P4) three times.
Rnd 3: P8, (K2, P6) two times, K4, P4, (K2, P6) two times, K2, P4.
Rnd 4: P2, (P4, 2/2 RPC) three times, K2, (P4, 2/2 LPC) three times, P2.
Rnd 5: (P6, K2) three times, P2, (K2, P6) three times, K2, P2.
Rnd 6: (P4, 2/2 RPC) three times, P2, 2/2 LC, (P4, 2/2 LPC) two times, P5, K1, P2.
Rnd 7: P4, (K2, P6) two times, K2, P4, K4, (P6, K2) two times, P8.
Rnd 8: P2, (2/2 RPC, P4) three times, K2, (2/2 LPC, P4) three times, P2.

Center Cable—Size 46.25" (flat over 66 sts)
Row 1 (WS): K4, (P2, K6) three times, P2, K2, (P2, K6) four times, K2.
Row 2 (RS): P6, (2/2 RPC, P4) three times, 2/2 RC, P2, (2/2 LPC, P4) three times, 2/2 LPC, P2.
Row 3: K2, (P2, K6) three times, P2, K4, P4, (K6, P2) three times, K6.
Row 4: (P4, 2/2 RPC) four times, K2, (P4, 2/2 LPC) three times, P5, K1, P2.
Row 5: K2, (K6, P2) four times, K2, (P2, K6) three times, P2, K4.
Row 6: P2, (2/2 RPC, P4) three times, 2/2 RPC, P2, 2/2 LC, (P4, 2/2 LPC) three times, P6.
Row 7: (K6, P2) four times, P2, K4, (P2, K6) three times, P2, K2.
Row 8: P2, K1, P5, (2/2 RPC, P4) three times, K2, (2/2 LPC, P4) four times.

Center Cable—Size 46.25" (in the round over 66 sts)
Rnd 1: P2, (P6, K2) four times, P2, (K2, P6) three times, K2, P4.
Rnd 2: P6, (2/2 RPC, P4) three times, 2/2 RC, P2, (2/2 LPC, P4) three times, 2/2 LPC, P2
Rnd 3: (P6, K2) four times, K2, P4, (K2, P6) three times, K2, P2.
Rnd 4: (P4, 2/2 RPC) four times, K2, (P4, 2/2 LPC) three times, P5, K1, P2.
Rnd 5: P4, (K2, P6) three times, K2, P2, (K2, P6) four times, P2.
Rnd 6: P2, (2/2 RPC, P4) three times, 2/2 RPC, P2, 2/2 LC, (P4, 2/2 LPC) three times, P6.
Rnd 7: P2, (K2, P6) three times, K2, P4, K4, (P6, K2) three times, P6.
Rnd 8: P2, K1, P5, (2/2 RPC, P4) three times, K2, (2/2 LPC, P4) four times.

Center Cable—Size 51.25" (flat over 78 sts)
Row 1 (WS): K2, (P2, K6) four times, P2, K2, (P2, K6) five times.
Row 2 (RS): (P4, 2/2 RPC), four times, P4, 2/2 RC, P2, (2/2 LPC, P4) four times, P1, K1, P2.
Row 3: K2, (K6, P2) four times, K4, P4, (K6, P2) four times, K4.
Row 4: P2, (2/2 RPC, P4) four times, 2/2 RPC, K2, (P4, 2/2 LPC) four times, P6.
Row 5: (K6, P2) five times, K2, (P2, K6) four times, P2, K2.
Row 6: P2, K1, P1, (P4, 2/2 RPC) four times, P2, 2/2 LC, (P4, 2/2 LPC) four times, P4.
Row 7: K4, (P2, K6) four times, P4, K4, (P2, K6) four times, K2.
Row 8: P2, (P4, 2/2 RPC) four times, P4, K2, (2/2 LPC, P4) four times, 2/2 LPC, P2.

Center Cable—Size 51.25" (in the round over 78 sts)
Rnd 1: (P6, K2) five times, P2, (K2, P6) four times, K2, P2.
Rnd 2: (P4, 2/2 RPC) four times, P4, 2/2 RC, P2, (2/2 LPC, P4) four times, P1, K1, P2.
Rnd 3: P4, (K2, P6) four times, K4, P4, (K2, P6) four times, P2.
Rnd 4: P2, (2/2 RPC, P4) four times, 2/2 RPC, K2, (P4, 2/2 LPC) four times, P6.
Rnd 5: P2, (K2, P6) four times, K2, P2, (K2, P6) five times.
Rnd 6: P2, K1, P1, (P4, 2/2 RPC) four times, P2, 2/2 LC, (P4, 2/2 LPC) four times, P4.
Rnd 7: P2, (P6, K2) four times, P4, K4, (P6, K2) four times, P4.
Rnd 8: P2, (P4, 2/2 RPC) four times, P4, K2, (2/2 LPC, P4) four times, 2/2 LPC, P2.

DIRECTIONS

Body

Hem & Bottom
CO 188 (208, 232, 252, 276) sts. PM and join to work in the rnd, being careful not to twist.
Work 2x2 Rib for 2".
Work St st until sweater measures 10 (10, 10.5, 11, 11)" from CO edge.

Begin Patterned Section
Rnds 1-2: P all.
Rnds 3-4: K all.
Rnds 5-6: P all.
Rnd 7: K all.

Size 34.5" Only
Setup Rnd: *P13, PM, K6, PM, K2, (M1L, K2) four times, PM, K6, PM, K2, (M1L, K3) seven times, PM, K6, PM, K2, (M1L, K2) four times, PM, K6, PM, P14*, PM to denote RH side of sweater; rep from * to * for back half. 218 total sts.

Size 38.75" Only
Setup Rnd: *P14, PM, K6, PM, K2, (M1L, K2) four times, PM, K6, PM, K2, (M1L, K3) nine times, M1L, K2, M1L, PM, K6, PM, K2, (M1L, K2) four times, PM, K6, PM, P15*, PM to denote RH side of sweater; rep from * to * for back half. 246 total sts.

Size 42.25" Only
Setup Rnd: *P14, PM, K6, PM, K2, (M1L, K2) four times, PM, K6, PM, K3, (M1L, K4) ten times, M1L, PM, K6, PM, K2, (M1L, K2) four times, PM, K6, PM, P15*, PM to denote RH side of sweater; rep from * to * for back half. 270 total sts.

Size 46.25" Only
Setup Rnd: *P15, PM, K6, PM, K2, (M1L, K2) four times, PM, K6, PM, K6, (M1L, K3) 15 times, PM, K6, PM, K2, (M1L, K2) four times, PM, K6, PM, P16*, PM to denote RH side of sweater; rep from * to * for back half. 298 total sts.

Size 51.25" Only
Setup Rnd: *P17, PM, K6, PM, K2, (M1L, K2) four times, PM, K6, PM, K2, (M1L, K3) 19 times, PM, K6, PM, K2, (M1L, K2) four times, PM, K6, PM, P18*, PM to denote RH side of sweater; rep from * to * for back half. 330 total sts.

All Sizes Resume
Note: Use stitch pattern instructions for working in the rnd.
Next Rnd: *P13 (14, 14, 15, 17), SM, Work Rnd 1 of Welts pattern, SM, Work Rnd 1 of Open Cable pattern, SM, Work Rnd 1 of Welts pattern, SM, Work Rnd 1 of Center Cable pattern for your size, SM, Work Rnd 1 of Welts pattern, SM, Work Rnd 1 of Open Cable pattern, SM, Work Rnd 1 of Welts pattern, SM, P14 (15, 15, 16, 18); rep from * for back half.
Work in pattern as established, repeating charts or written instructions until sweater measures 16.5 (17, 18, 18.5, 19)" from CO edge, or desired length, ending with an even-numbered pattern rnd.

Separate Sleeves: *Work across front half in pattern (working odd-numbered pattern rows for each pattern section), P to 6 (7, 7, 8, 10) sts before side M, BO 11 (13, 13, 15, 19) underarm sts; rep from * for back half.

Front Yoke

Begin working flat over 98 (110, 122, 134, 146) sts for front half of sweater only, using stitch pattern instructions for working flat. Move back sts to scrap yarn or a spare needle. Working an even-numbered pattern row (RS row), cont in pattern as follows:
Underarm Shaping Row (RS): P1, P2tog, work Rev St st to M, work in pattern across front, work Rev St st to 3 sts from end, P2tog, P1. 96 (108, 120, 132, 144) sts.
Next Row (WS): Work Rev St st to M, work in pattern across all sts to last M, work Rev St st to end.
Rep last two rows five more times. 86 (98, 110, 122, 134) sts.

Cont to work even in pattern until front half measures 5.75 (6.25, 6.75, 7.25, 7.75)" from underarm; end on a WS row.

Front Neck Shaping Setup Row (RS): Work in pattern to Center Cable, SM, work in pattern for 3 (7, 11, 16, 21) sts, BO 24 (28, 32, 34, 36) sts, cont in pattern across remaining Center Cable sts, then cont in pattern to end of row.
Move LH yoke/shoulder sts to scrap yarn or a st holder.

Right-Hand Front Yoke
Row 1 (WS): Working RH side of front only, work in pattern to end. 31 (35, 39, 44, 49) sts.
Row 2: BO 3 (3, 4, 5, 5) sts, work in pattern to end. 28 (32, 35, 39, 44) sts.
Row 3: Work in pattern to end.
Row 4: BO 2 sts, work in pattern to end. 26 (30, 33, 37, 42) sts.
Row 5: Work in pattern to end.
Row 6: Dec 1 st at neck edge, work in pattern to end. 25 (29, 32, 36, 41) sts.
Rep Rows 5-6 once more. 24 (28, 31, 35, 40) sts.

Cont to work even in pattern until front RH piece measures approx 8 (8.5, 9, 9.5, 10)" from underarm; end on a RS row.

Short Row Shoulder Shaping
Row 1 (WS): Work in pattern to end.
Short Row 2 (RS): Work in pattern to 6 (6, 7, 8, 9) sts from end, turn to work in opposite direction, work German Short Row.
Short Row 3: Work in pattern to end.

Short Row 4: Work in pattern to 12 (13, 15, 17, 19) sts from end, turn, work German Short Row.
Short Row 5: Work in pattern to end.
Row 6: Work in pattern across all sts; when you reach the twisted, two-legged sts that resulted from German Short Rows, work in pattern as well.
Do not BO. Transfer sts to scrap yarn or a st holder. Break yarn.

Left-Hand Front Yoke
Return 31 (35, 39, 44, 49) LH yoke/shoulder sts to needles.
Row 1 (WS): With WS facing, rejoin yarn and BO 3 (3, 4, 5, 5) sts, work in pattern to end. 28 (32, 35, 39, 44) sts.
Row 2 (RS): Work in pattern to end.
Row 3: BO 2 sts, work in pattern to end. 26 (30, 33, 37, 42) sts.
Row 4: Work in pattern to end.
Row 5: Dec 1 st at neck edge, work in pattern to end. 25 (29, 32, 36, 41) sts.
Rep Rows 4-5 once more. 24 (28, 31, 35, 40) sts.

Cont to work even in pattern until front LH piece measures approx 8 (8.5, 9, 9.5, 10)" from underarm; end on a RS row.

Short Row Shoulder Shaping
Short Row 1 (WS): Work in pattern to 6 (6, 7, 8, 9) sts from end, turn to work in opposite direction, work German Short Row.
Short Row 2 (RS): Work in pattern to end.
Short Row 3: Work in pattern to 12 (13, 15, 17, 19) sts from end, work German Short Row.
Short Row 4: Work in pattern to end.
Row 5: Work in pattern across all sts; when you reach the twisted, two-legged sts that resulted from German Short Rows, work in pattern as well.
Do not BO. Transfer sts to scrap yarn or a st holder. Break yarn.

Back Yoke
Return 98 (110, 122, 134, 146) back sts to needles. With RS facing, rejoin yarn and work Underarm Shaping Rows same as for front half of sweater. 86 (98, 110, 122, 134) sts.

Cont to work even in pattern until back yoke measures approx 7.5 (8, 8.5, 9, 9.5)" from underarm; end on a WS row.

Back Neck Setup Row (RS): Work in pattern to Center Cable, SM, work in pattern for 3 (7, 11, 16, 21) sts, BO 24 (28, 32, 34, 36) sts, cont in pattern across remaining Center Cable sts, then cont in pattern to end of row. Move RH yoke/shoulder sts to scrap yarn or a st holder.

Left-Hand Back Yoke
Row 1 (WS): Working LH side of back only, work in pattern to end. 31 (35, 39, 44, 49) sts.
Row 2: BO 3 (3, 4, 5, 5) sts, work in pattern to end. 28 (32, 35, 39, 44) sts.
Row 3: Work in pattern to end.
Row 4: BO 2 sts, work in pattern to end. 26 (30, 33, 37, 42) sts.
Row 5: Work in pattern to end.
Short Row 6: Dec 1 st at neck edge, work in pattern to 6 (6, 7, 8, 9) sts before end, turn, work German Short Row. 25 (29, 32, 36, 41) sts.
Short Row 7: Work in pattern to end.
Short Row 8: Dec 1 st at neck edge, work in pattern to 12 (13, 15, 17, 19) sts before end, turn, work German Short Row. 24 (28, 31, 35, 40) sts.
Short Row 9: Work in pattern to end.
Row 10: Work across in pattern, working short row sts in pattern as for front half.
Do not BO. Transfer sts to scrap yarn or a st holder. Break yarn leaving 18" long tail.

Right-Hand Back Yoke
Return 31 (35, 39, 44, 49) RH yoke/shoulder sts to needles.
Row 1 (WS): With WS facing, rejoin yarn and BO 3 (3, 4, 5, 5) sts, work in pattern to end. 28 (32, 35, 39, 44) sts.
Row 2 (RS): Work in pattern to end.
Row 3: BO 2 sts, work in pattern to end. 26 (30, 33, 37, 42) sts.
Row 4: Work in pattern to end.
Short Row 5: Dec 1 st at neck edge, work in pattern to 6 (6, 7, 8, 9) sts before end, turn, work German Short Row. 25 (29, 32, 36, 41) sts.
Short Row 6: Work in pattern to end.
Short Row 7: Dec 1 st at neck edge, work in pattern to 12 (13, 15, 17, 19) sts before end, turn, work German Short Row. 24 (28, 31, 35, 40) sts.
Short Row 8: Work in pattern to end.
Row 9: Work across in pattern, working short row sts in pattern as for front half.
Do not BO and do not break yarn.

Join Front to Back
Transfer RH front shoulder sts to a DPN or spare needle, hold parallel to RH back shoulder sts, RSs facing inward and WSs facing outward. Use working yarn still attached to back RH shoulder and work 3-Needle Bind Off to join.

Transfer LH front shoulder sts and LH back shoulder sts each to their own DPN or spare needle, hold parallel, RSs facing inward and WSs facing outward. Use the 18" tail left on back LH shoulder and work 3-Needle Bind Off to join.

Sleeves (make two the same)
Before picking up sts around armhole, place 2 removable Ms 1" down from 3-Needle Bind Off at top of shoulder—one on front side and one on back side.

Using preferred needles for working small circumferences in the rnd, begin picking up sleeve sts as follows: with RS facing, and beginning at center of underarm, PU and K 5 (6, 6, 7, 9) sts over half of underarm BO sts, evenly PU and K 29 (30, 32, 34, 38) sts between corner of underarm and removable M, PU and K 7 sts between removable M and top of shoulder, PM, PU and K 7 sts between top of shoulder and next removable M, evenly PU and K 29 (30, 32, 34, 38) sts between removable M and corner of underarm, PU and K 5 (6, 6, 7, 9) sts over remaining half of underarm BO sts, PM for BOR. Remove the removable Ms from front and back of sweater. 82 (86, 90, 96, 108) total sts.

Short Row Sleeve Cap Shaping
Setup Row (RS): P to 13 sts before M at top of shoulder, PM, K6, PM, K7, remove M, K7, PM, K1, turn, work German Short Row as for Shoulder Shaping sections.
Short Row 1 (WS): SM, work Row 1 of Open Cable pattern (follow instructions for working flat), SM, P1, turn, work German Short Row.
Short Row 2 (RS): SM, work Row 2 of Open Cable pattern, SM, K short row st from previous row, K5, PM, P1 (2, 3, 4, 5), turn, work German Short Row.
Short Row 3: K0 (1, 2, 3, 4), SM, Work Row 1 of Welts pattern (follow instructions for working flat), SM, Work Row 3 of Open Cable pattern, SM, K short row st from previous row, K5, SM, K1 (2, 3, 4, 5), turn, work German Short Row.
Short Row 4: Work Rev St st (following instructions for working flat) to M, SM, work next row of Welts pattern, SM, work next row of Open Cable pattern, SM, work next row of Welts pattern, SM, work Rev St st to short row st from previous row, P that st, P1, turn, work German Short Row.
Short Row 5: Work in Rev St st to M, SM, work next row of Welts pattern, SM, work next row of Open Cable pattern, SM, work next row of Welts pattern, SM, work in Rev St st to short row st from previous row, K that st, K1, turn, work German Short Row.
Rep Short Rows 4-5, continuing to work Welts and Open Cable sections in pattern, until only 13 (13, 12, 11, 13) sts remain on either side of BOR M, ending with an odd-numbered (WS) row.

Dec Short Row (RS): P1, P2tog, work in pattern to 3 sts before short row st from previous row, P2tog, P1, P short row st, P1, turn, work German Short Row. 80 (84, 88, 94, 106) sts.
Next Short Row (WS): Work as for Short Row 5.
Rep last two rows 5 (4, 3, 1, 1) more time(s), ending with an odd-numbered (WS) row. Only 7 (8, 8, 9, 11) sts remain on either side of BOR M. 70 (76, 82, 92, 104) sts.

Next Rnd (RS): Work in pattern to short row st from previous rnd, P that st, then P to end of rnd.
From this point on, sleeve will be worked in the rnd.
Work 11 (10, 9, 7, 5) rnds in pattern (following stitch pattern instructions for working in the rnd). Note: P last short row st on the first of these rnds.
Sleeve Dec Rnd: P1, P2tog, work in pattern to 3 sts before BOR M, P2tog, P1. 68 (74, 80, 90, 102) sts.
Work 11 (10, 9, 7, 5) rnds even in pattern.
Rep last 12 (11, 10, 8, 6) rnds 2 (3, 4, 5, 8) more times.
Work even in pattern until sleeve measures approx 5.75 (6.25, 6.75, 6.75, 7.25)" from underarm, ending with Row 2 of Welts pattern. 64 (68, 72, 80, 86) sts.

Next Rnd: K to M, remove M, K6, remove M, K2 (K2tog, K1) four times, remove M, K6, remove M, K to M. 60 (64, 68, 76, 82) sts.
Next Rnd: K all.
Next Rnd: P all.
Next Rnd: P all.
Next Rnd: K all.
Next Rnd: K all.
Next Rnd: P all.
Next Rnd: P all.
Sleeve Dec Rnd: K, K2tog, K to 3 sts before M, SSK, K1. 58 (62, 66, 74, 80) sts.
Work St st, and cont working most recent Sleeve Dec Rnd every 11 (10, 10, 8, 6) rnds 7 (7, 7, 9, 10) more times. 11 (12, 13, 16, 20) total dec rnds (including the ones worked in upper sleeve section) have been completed. 44 (48, 52, 56, 60) sts.

Work St st until sleeve measures approx 18 (18, 18.5, 18.5, 19)" from underarm, or 2" shorter than desired length.
Work 2x2 Rib for 2".
BO loosely in pattern.

Turtleneck
Using 16" long circular needles, with RS facing, beginning at top of RH shoulder, PU and K 6 sts down RH side of back neck, PU and K 32 (34, 36, 40, 40) sts across bottom of back neck, PU and K 6 sts up LH side of back neck, PU and K 20 sts down LH side of front neck, PU and K 32 (34, 36, 40, 40) sts across bottom of front neck, PU and K 20 sts up RH side of front neck. PM and join to work in the rnd. 116 (120, 124, 132, 132) total sts.
Work 2x2 Rib for 5".
BO loosely in pattern.

Finishing
Weave in ends, wash, and block to diagram.

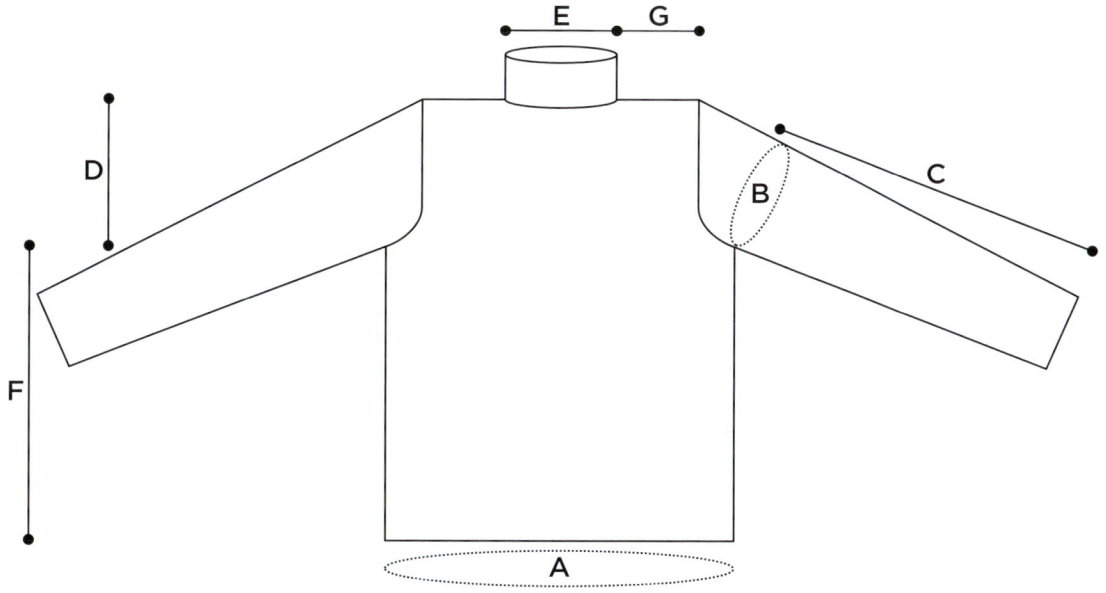

A 34.5 (38.75, 42.25, 46.25, 51.25)"

B 12 (13.25, 14.25, 16, 18.25)"

C 20 (20, 20.5, 20.5, 21)"

D 8 (8.5, 9, 9.5, 10)"

E 5.75 (6, 6.75, 7.5, 7.75)"

F 16.5 (17, 18, 18.5, 19)"

G 3.5 (4.25, 5, 5.5, 6)"

LEGEND

☐ **K**
RS: Knit stitch
WS: Purl stitch

⊡ **P**
RS: Purl stitch
WS: Knit stitch

Ⅴ **Sl**
RS: Slip stitch purl-wise, with yarn in back
WS: Slip stitch purl-wise, with yarn in front

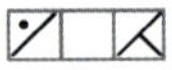

Cable 2 Over 1 Right, Purl back (2/1 RPC)
Sl1 to CN, hold in back; K2, P1 from CN

Cable 2 Over 1 Left, Purl back (2/1 LPC)
Sl2 to CN, hold in front; P1, K2 from CN

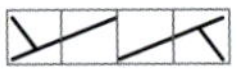

Cable 2 Over 2 Right (2/2 RC)
Sl2 to CN, hold in back; K2, K2 from CN

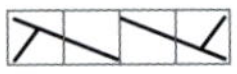

Cable 2 Over 2 Left (2/2 LC)
Sl2 to CN, hold in front; K2, K2 from CN

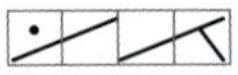

Cable 2 Over 2 Right, Purl back (2/2 RPC)
Sl2 to CN, hold in back; K2, P2 from CN

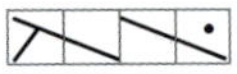

Cable 2 Over 2 Left, Purl back (2/2 LPC)
Sl2 to CN, hold in front; P2, K2 from CN

□ **Pattern Repeat**

Welts

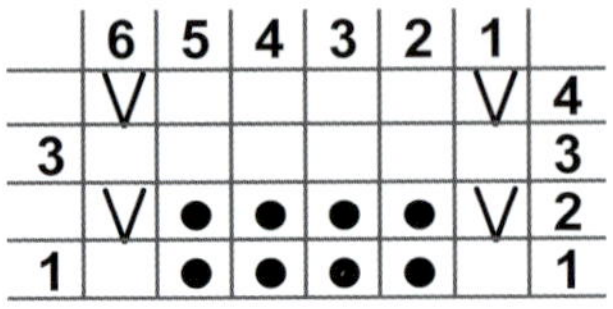

6	5	4	3	2	1	
Ⅴ				Ⅴ		4
						3
Ⅴ	•	•	•	Ⅴ		2
	•	•	•			1

Open Cable

(14-stitch × 14-row chart)

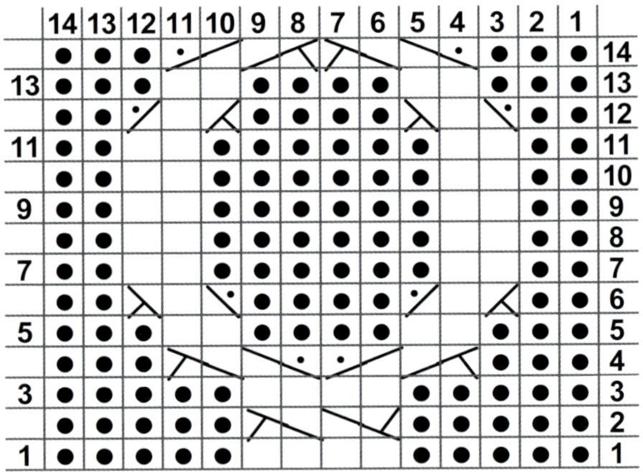

Center Cable—Size 34.5"

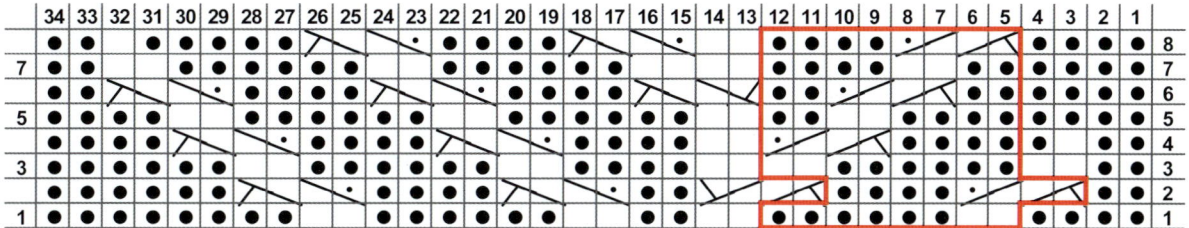

Center Cable—Size 38.75"

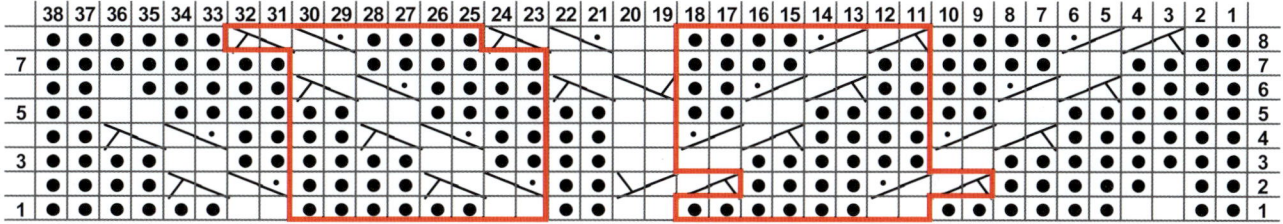

Work rep sts two times total

Center Cable—Size 42.25"

Work rep sts two times total

Center Cable—Size 46.25"

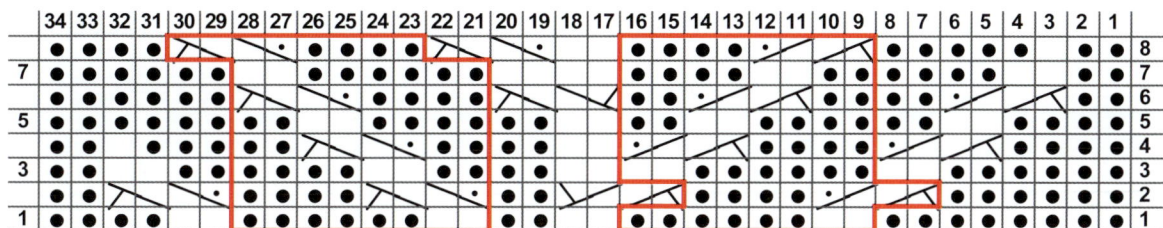

Work rep sts three times total

Center Cable—Size 51.25"

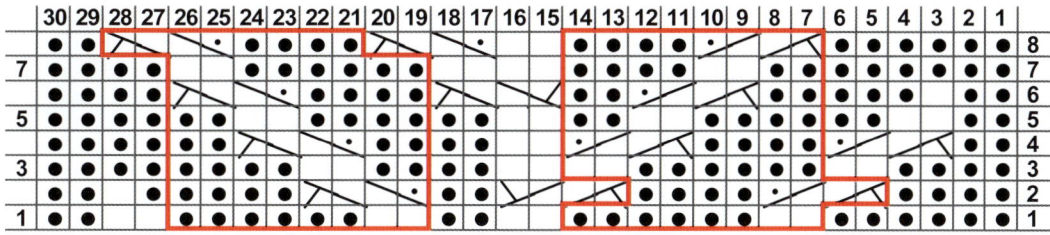

Work rep sts four times total

Gray Days

JETTY

by Renate Kamm

FINISHED MEASUREMENTS
32 (34, 38, 42, 46, 50)" finished chest circumference (measured just below the gussets); meant to be worn with 2-3" positive ease

YARN
Knit Picks Wool of the Andes™ (sport weight, 100% Peruvian Highland Wool; 137 yards/50g): Sapphire Heather 25291, 10 (10, 11, 13, 14, 15) skeins

NEEDLES
US 4 (3.5mm) 16" and 32" circular needles and DPNs, or size to obtain gauge
US 3 (3.25mm) straight needles or 32" circular needles, and 16" circular needles, and a set of DPNs, or one size smaller than size used to obtain gauge

NOTIONS
Yarn Needle
Removable Stitch Markers
Cable Needle
Scrap Yarn or Stitch Holders
Spare DPNs

GAUGE
24 sts and 34 rnds = 4" in Stockinette Stitch in the round with larger needles, blocked

For pattern support, contact oberpfalzerin@hotmail.com

Jetty

Notes:

To honor the past work of the knitters of Guernsey Island, Jetty is packed with many traditional elements that originate from that historical island life. For the fisherman back then, the garment needed to be wool and well-fitted. To accomplish this, the knitters developed practical traditions, such as an overlapping hem, underarm gussets, straight line edges, seamless bottom-up construction, saddle shoulders, seamless in-the-round sleeves, straight neck, and stand-up collar.

Besides all this purposeful tradition, Jetty also mirrors the artful patterning of that time, with a fresh design across the chest and portions of it repeated on the upper sleeves.

Some stitch patterns are written and charted. Charts are worked both flat and in the round. When working charts in the round, read each chart row from right to left as a RS row. When working charts flat, read RS rows (odd numbers) from right to left, and WS rows (even numbers) from left to right.

Channel Island Cast On

Prepare a tail as for Long Tail Cast On. Double the length of that tail and fold in half. Make a slip knot and slip it onto RH needle, with double tail on one side and open end of folded tail and working yarn with ball attached on other side.

The single strand with working yarn attached is placed over the left index finger and the double tail is wrapped counter clockwise twice around the left thumb; the short tail is hanging free.

Step 1: Bring needle over single strand on index finger to make a YO. Be sure to wrap yarn front to back to create YO.

Step 2: Bring needle up through the 2 doubled strands on thumb, grab a loop of single strand as if to knit, then bring needle back down through loops on thumb. Be sure to put needle through both wraps and both strands when picking up stitch of single strand.

Step 3: Release wraps from thumb, and pull gently to snug up st. At the same time, wrap doubled tail counterclockwise twice around thumb in preparation to begin again. 2 sts have been cast on.

Rep Steps 1-3 for desired number of sts. When counting sts, treat loops of slip knot as 2 sts for an even number of sts. For a tutorial, visit https://tutorials.knitpicks.com/channel-islands-cast-on.

Jeny's Surprisingly Stretchy BO

Processing a K st: Wrap yarn around RH needle in a reverse YO, from back to front. K 1 st. Pull YO over K st.

Processing a P st: Wrap yarn around RH needle in a YO, from front to back. P 1 st. Pull YO over P st.

BO Step 1: Process first st as described above; 1 st on the RH needle.

BO Step 2: Process next st as described above.

BO Step 3: Pull first st on RH needle over second st on RH needle and off needle.

Repeat Steps 2-3 until 1 st remains. Cut yarn to 4" and pull through last st.

Cable 2 Over 2 Right (2/2 RC)
Sl2 to CN, hold in back; K2, K2 from CN.

Cable 2 Over 2 Left (2/2 LC)
Sl2 to CN, hold in front; K2, K2 from CN.

Right Yoke Texture (worked flat)
Row 1 (RS): K1 (edge st), (K1, P1) for the set amount of sts.
Row 2 (WS): Work sts as they appear (K the knit sts, P the purl sts) to last st, Sl1 (edge st).
Row 3: K1 (edge st), (P1, K1) for the set amount of sts.
Row 4: Work sts as they appear (K the knit sts, P the purl sts) to last st, Sl1 (edge st).
Rep Rows 1-4 for pattern.

Left Yoke Texture (worked flat)
Row 1 (RS): (K1, P1) for the set amount of sts to last st, K1 (edge st).
Row 2 (WS): Sl1 (edge st), work sts as they appear (K the knit sts, P the purl sts) for the set amount of sts.
Row 3: (P1, K1) for the set amount of sts to last st, K1 (edge st).
Row 4: Sl1 (edge st), work sts as they appear (K the knit sts, P the purl sts) for the set amount of sts.
Rep Rows 1-4 for pattern.

Right Yoke Texture (in the round)
Rnd 1: K1, (K1, P1) for the set amount of sts.
Rnd 2: P1, work sts as they appear (K the knit sts, P the purl sts) for the set amount of sts.
Rnd 3: K1, (P1, K1) for the set amount of sts.
Rnd 4: P1, work sts as they appear (K the knit sts, P the purl sts) for the set amount of sts.
Rep Rnds 1-4 for pattern.

Left Yoke Texture (in the round)
Rnd 1: (K1, P1) for the set amount of sts to last st, K1.
Rnd 2: Work sts as they appear (K the knit sts, P the purl sts) to last st, P1.
Rnd 3: (P1, K1) for the set amount of sts to last st, K1.
Rnd 4: Work sts as they appear (K the knit sts, P the purl sts) to last st, P1.
Rep Rnds 1-4 for pattern.

Large Horn Cable (flat over 16 sts)
Row 1 (RS): K4, 2/2 RC, 2/2 LC, K4.
Row 2 (WS): P16.
Row 3: K2, 2/2 RC, K4, 2/2 LC, K2.
Row 4: P16.
Row 5: 2/2 RC, K8, 2/2 LC.
Row 6: P16.
Rep Rows 1-6 for pattern.

Large Horn Cable (in the round over 16 sts)
Rnd 1: K4, 2/2 RC, 2/2 LC, K4.
Rnd 2: K16.
Rnd 3: K2, 2/2 RC, K4, 2/2 LC, K2.
Rnd 4: K16.

Rnd 5: 2/2 RC, K8, 2/2 LC.
Rnd 6: K16.
Rep Rnds 1-6 for pattern.

Yoke Diamonds (flat over 13 sts)
Row 1 (RS): K13.
Row 2 (WS): P6, K1, P6.
Row 3: K5, P1, K1, P1, K5.
Row 4: P4, (K1, P1) three times, P3.
Row 5: K3, (P1, K1) four times, K2.
Row 6: P2, (K1, P1) five times, P1.
Row 7: K1, (P1, K1) six times.
Row 8: Rep Row 6.
Row 9: Rep Row 5.
Row 10: Rep Row 4.
Row 11: Rep Row 3.
Row 12: Rep Row 2.
Row 13: Rep Row 1.
Row 14: Rep Row 2.
Row 15: K5, P3, K5.
Row 16: P4, K5, P4.
Row 17: K3, P7, K3.
Row 18: P2, K9, P2.
Row 19: K1, P11, K1.
Row 20: Rep Row 18.
Row 21: Rep Row 17.
Row 22: Rep Row 16.
Row 23: Rep Row 15.
Row 24: Rep Row 2.
Rep Rows 1-24 for pattern.

Yoke Diamonds (in the round over 13 sts)
Rnd 1: K13.
Rnd 2: K6, P1, K6.
Rnd 3: K5, P1, K1, P1, K5.
Rnd 4: K4, (P1, K1) three times, K3.
Rnd 5: K3, (P1, K1) four times, K2.
Rnd 6: K2, (P1, K1) five times, K1.
Rnd 7: K1, (P1, K1) six times.
Rnd 8: Rep Rnd 6.
Rnd 9: Rep Rnd 5.
Rnd 10: Rep Rnd 4.
Rnd 11: Rep Rnd 3.
Rnd 12: Rep Rnd 2.
Rnd 13: Rep Rnd 1.
Rnd 14: Rep Rnd 2.
Rnd 15: K5, P3, K5.
Rnd 16: K4, P5, K4.
Rnd 17: K3, P7, K3.
Rnd 18: K2, P9, K2.
Rnd 19: K1, P11, K1.
Rnd 20: Rep Rnd 18.
Rnd 21: Rep Rnd 17.
Rnd 22: Rep Rnd 16.
Rnd 23: Rep Rnd 15.
Rnd 24: Rep Rnd 2.
Rep Rnds 1-24 for pattern.

Sleeve Diamonds (in the round over 24 sts; rep around sleeve, see chart for which st to start with for your size)
Rnd 1: K all.
Rnd 2: K6, P1, K11, P1, K5.
Rnd 3: K5, P1, K1, P1, K9, P3, K4.
Rnd 4: K4, (P1, K1) three times, K6, P5, K3.
Rnd 5: K3, (P1, K1) four times, K4, P7, K2.
Rnd 6: K2, (P1, K1) five times, K2, P9, K1.
Rnd 7: K1, (P1, K1) six times, P9.
Rnd 8: Rep Rnd 6.
Rnd 9: Rep Rnd 5.
Rnd 10: Rep Rnd 4.
Rnd 11: Rep Rnd 3.
Rnd 12: Rep Rnd 2.

DIRECTIONS

Hem
With smaller straight or circular needles CO 86 (92, 102, 114, 124, 136) sts using the Channel Island Cast On method. Knit 10 (10, 10, 12, 12, 12) rows.
Cut working yarn, leaving 4" tail. Move sts to 32" long larger circular needles, with tail end on right side of sts.
Rep from * to * once more.
Move the sts to the same larger circular needles, so that cut tail from first hem section is in the middle and working yarn from second hem section is at the right side, the beginning of sts on LH needle.
Close rnd with overlapping sts as follows, careful not to twist the two garter hem sections: Sl2 sts from RH needle to CN, hold in back, (Sl1 from LH needle to RH needle, Sl1 from CN to RH needle) two times, Sl1 from LH needle; 5 sts are now overlapping on RH needle. Working across first hem section, K4 (7, 6, 12, 11, 17) *KFB, K5; rep from * 11 (11, 13, 13, 15, 15) more times, K to last 3 sts of first hem section, Sl3 to CN, hold in front, (Sl1 from CN to RH needle, Sl1 from LH needle [second hem section]) two times, Sl1 from CN; slide all 5 overlap sts back to LH needle, SSK twice, PM to mark side edge, K1, working across second hem section K4 (7, 6, 12, 11, 17), *KFB, K5; rep from * 11 (11, 13, 13, 15, 15) more times, K to first overlap st, K1, PM for BOR and side edge, K2tog twice. The rnd is now closed with both hem sections overlapping (front piece is overlapping back piece on both sides).
192 (204, 228, 252, 276, 300) sts.

Body
Work St st in the rnd for 92 (97, 97, 97, 101, 101) rnds, or approx 1.5 (1.5, 1.5, 2, 2, 2.25)" shorter than desired length for arm opening.

Underarm Gussets & Yoke
The next five rnds are worked in Garter st in the rnd and sts are inc for gussets. First inc rnd establishes center gusset st. Every following inc rnd adds 2 sts, one each side of center.
Rnd 1 (Setup Rnd): SM, M1R, PM, P to M, SM, M1L, PM, P to end. 194 (206, 230, 254, 278, 302) sts.
Rnd 2: K all.
Rnd 3: P all.

Rnd 4 (Inc Rnd): SM, M1R, work in pattern to M, M1L, SM, K to M, SM, M1R, K to M, M1L, SM, work in pattern to end. 4 sts inc.
Rnd 5: SM, K to M, SM, work in pattern to M, SM, K to M, work in pattern to end.
Rnd 6: *SM, K to M (gusset sts), SM, work Right Yoke Texture (in the rnd) over 11 (14, 20, 26, 32, 38) sts, K2, P2, work Yoke Diamonds (in the rnd) starting with Rnd 7 (7, 1, 1, 7, 1), (P2, K1) three times, P3, work Large Horn Cable (in the rnd) starting with Rnd 1, P3, (K1, P2) three times, work Yoke Diamond (in the rnd) starting with Rnd 7 (7, 1, 1, 7, 1), P2, K2, work Left Yoke Texture (in the rnd) over 11 (14, 20, 26, 32, 38) sts; rep from * once more.

Cont patterns as established and work Inc Rnd every third rnd 3 (3, 3, 4, 4, 5) more times. 210 (222, 246, 274, 298, 326) sts total; 9 (9, 11, 11, 13) sts each side underarm gusset.
Work 6 (6, 6, 9, 9, 6) rnds even in established pattern after final Inc Rnd.

Yoke is now worked separately and both Front and Back Yoke are worked flat with 1 edge st on each edge.
Division Rnd: Remove M, K9 (9, 9, 11, 11, 13) sts, Sl these just worked gusset sts onto a st holder or scrap yarn, cont as established in pattern to M, Sl next 9 (9, 11, 11, 13) gusset sts onto a st holder or scrap yarn, Sl remaining 96 (102, 114, 126, 138, 150) sts for Back Yoke to st holder or scrap yarn.

Front Yoke
Front is now worked flat, starting with a WS row.
Work as established in pattern for 56 (56, 62, 68, 74, 78) more rows.
Knit four rows.
Next Row (WS): Sl1, K3 (2, 3, 3, 6, 6), *K2tog, K1; rep from * 8 (9, 10, 12, 13, 15) more times and place these 22 (23, 26, 30, 35, 39) shoulder sts on a holder, K34 (36, 40, 40, 40, 40) and place these neck sts on a holder, *K1, K2tog, rep from * 8 (9, 10, 12, 13, 15) more times, K3 (2, 3, 3, 6, 6), Sl1 and place these 22 (23, 26, 30, 35, 39) shoulder sts on a holder.
61 (61, 67, 73, 79, 83) rows have been worked from the point of separation. Approx total garment length 21.25 (21.75, 22.5, 23.75, 25, 25.25)".

Back Yoke
Work Back same as Front.

Saddles
Left Saddle
Place Left Back Yoke sts and Left Front Yoke sts on small straight needles with points of needles pointing toward neck. With RS facing and scrap yarn in a contrasting color, provisionally CO 18 (18, 18, 22, 22, 22) sts onto the needle holding the Left Front Yoke sts.
Still using scrap yarn, with RS facing, knit these 18 (18, 18, 22, 22, 22) saddle sts onto needle holding Left Back Yoke sts. Break scrap yarn, turn.
Join main yarn below last st on RH needle and, with WS facing, purl the 18 (18, 18, 22, 22, 22) saddle sts onto needle holding Left Front Yoke sts.
Turn work so RSs of Left Front Yoke and Left Back Yoke pieces are facing. You now have 40 (41, 44, 52, 57, 61) sts on LH needle and 22 (23, 26, 30, 35, 39) sts on RH needle.

Sizes 32", 34" & 38" Only
Row 1 (RS): Sl1 K-wise WYIB, P1, (K1, P2) two times, K2 TBL, (P2, K1) two times, P1, SSK (1 st from saddle and 1 st from shoulder), turn.
Row 2 (WS): Sl1 P-wise WYIF, K1, (P1, K2) two times, P2, (K2, P1) two times, K1, P2tog (1 st from saddle and 1 st from shoulder), turn.

Sizes 42", 46" & 50" Only
Row 1 (RS): Sl1 K-wise WYIB, P1, K1, P1, (K1, P2) two times, K2 TBL, (P2, K1) two times, P1, K1, P1, SSK (1 st from saddle and 1 st from shoulder), turn.
Row 2 (WS): Sl1 P-wise WYIF, K1, P1, K1, (P1, K2) two times, P2, (K2, P1) two times, K1, P1, K1, P2tog (1 st from saddle and 1 st from shoulder), turn.

All Sizes Resume
Cont Left Saddle in pattern as established until all Left Back Yoke and all Left Front Yoke sts have been incorporated into saddle and 18 (18, 18, 22, 22, 22) sts remain.
Break yarn and place these 18 (18, 18, 22, 22, 22) sts on a holder.

Right Saddle
Place Right Back Yoke sts and Right Front Yoke sts on small straight needles with points of needles pointing toward neck. With RS facing and scrap yarn in a contrasting color, provisionally CO 18 (18, 18, 22, 22, 22) sts onto the needle holding the Right Back Yoke sts.
Still using scrap yarn, with RS facing, knit these 18 (18, 18, 22, 22, 22) saddle sts onto the needle holding the Right Front Yoke sts. Break scrap yarn, turn.
Join main yarn below last st on RH needle and, with WS facing, purl the 18 (18, 18, 22, 22, 22) saddle sts onto needle holding Right Front Yoke sts.
Turn work so RSs of Right Front Yoke and Right Back Yoke pieces are facing. You now have 40 (41, 44, 52, 57, 61) sts on LH needle and 22 (23, 26, 30, 35, 39) sts on RH needle.

Sizes 32", 34" & 38" Only
Row 1 (RS): Sl1 K-wise WYIB, P1, (K1, P2) two times, K2 TBL, (P2, K1) two times, P1, SSK (1 st from saddle and 1 st from shoulder), turn.
Row 2 (WS): Sl1 P-wise WYIF, K1, (P1, K2) two times, P2, (K2, P1) two times, K1, P2tog (1 st from saddle and 1 st from shoulder), turn.

Sizes 42", 46" & 50" Only
Row 1 (RS): Sl1 K-wise WYIB, P1, K1, P1, (K1, P2) two times, K2 TBL, (P2, K1) two times, P1, K1, P1, SSK (1 st from saddle and 1 st from shoulder), turn.
Row 2 (WS): Sl1 P-wise WYIF, K1, P1, K1, (P1, K2) two times, P2, (K2, P1) two times, K1, P1, K1, P2tog (1 st from saddle and 1 st from shoulder), turn.

All Sizes Resume
Cont Right Saddle in pattern as established until all Right Back Yoke and all Right Front Yoke sts have been incorporated into saddle and 18 (18, 18, 22, 22, 22) sts remain. Break yarn and place these 18 (18, 18, 22, 22, 22) sts on a st holder or scrap yarn.

Sleeves
Right Sleeve
With the 16" long larger circular needles and RS facing, K9 (9, 9, 11, 11, 13) held Gusset sts, PM, cont up Right Front Yoke PU and K 42 (42, 46, 48, 52, 56) sts, K18 (18, 18, 22, 22, 22) held Saddle sts, cont down Right Back Yoke, PU and K 42 (42, 46, 48, 52, 56) sts, PM for BOR. 111 (111, 119, 129, 137, 147) sts. The next five rnds are worked in Garter st in the rnd and sts are dec for gussets.
Rnd 1: K to M, SM, P to end.
Rnd 2: K all.
Rnd 3: K to M, SM, P to end.
Rnd 4 (Dec Rnd): SSK, K to 2 sts before M, K2tog, SM, work in pattern to end. 2 gusset sts dec between Ms.
Rnd 5: K to M, SM, work in pattern to end.
While working Sleeve in next section, cont to dec underarm gussets every third rnd 2 (2, 2, 3, 3, 4) more times; 3 gusset sts remain. Work two more rnds even, then CDD over 3 gusset sts; 1 gusset st remains. On the very next rnd, finish rnd with K2tog TBL to dec last gusset st; one of the Ms can now be removed.
Rnd 6: K to M, SM, work Sleeve Diamonds Row 1 for 50 (50, 54, 58, 64, 68) sts, K2tog, work Sleeve Diamonds Row 1 to end. 108 (108, 116, 126, 134, 144) sts.
Rnds 7-17: Working gusset decs as needed, starting with the correct st for your size, work Rnds 2-12 of Sleeve Diamonds.
Rnds 18-22: Working gusset decs as needed, work Garter st in the rnd, starting with a P rnd.
101 (101, 109, 117, 125, 133) sts after completing gusset decs.
Sleeve Dec Rnd: K1, SSK, work Right Yoke Texture to last 3 sts, K2tog, K1, SM. 2 sts dec; 99 (99, 107, 115, 123, 131) sts. Work eleven more rnds of Right Yoke Texture, then work five rnds of Garter st in the rnd, then work St st until sleeve measures 19 (18.5, 18.5, 18.25, 18)" from pick up rnd.
AT THE SAME TIME, rep Sleeve Dec Rnd, working appropriate pattern between decs, every eighth rnd 15 (14, 0, 0, 0, 0) times, every seventh rnd 0 (0, 18, 0, 0, 0) times, every sixth rnd 1 (2, 0, 18, 0, 0) times, every fifth rnd 0 (0, 1, 0, 20, 0) times, every fourth rnd 0 (0, 0, 5, 6, 30) times. Switch to DPNs as needed.
67 (67, 69, 69, 71, 71) sts.

Cuff
Next Rnd: *K2tog, K20 (20, 11, 11, 21, 21); rep from * 1 (1, 3, 3, 1, 1) more time(s), K2tog, K to end. 64 (64, 64, 64, 68, 68) sts. With smaller size DPNs, work 2x2 Rib until cuff measures 2 (2, 2, 2.25, 2.25, 2.5)".
BO all sts with Jeny's Surprisingly Stretchy Bind Off.

Left Sleeve
Work Left Sleeve same as for Right, using Left Yoke Texture pattern instead of Right Yoke Texture.

Neckband
With the 16" long size US 3 (3.25mm) circular needles and RS facing, place 34 (36, 40, 40, 40, 40) held back neck sts onto needle, remove provisional yarn and place 18 (18, 18, 22, 22, 22) right saddle sts onto needle, place 34 (36, 40, 40, 40, 40) held front neck sts onto needle, and remove provisional yarn and place 18 (18, 18, 22, 22, 22) left right saddle sts onto needle. 104 (108, 116, 124, 124, 124) sts.
Join to work in the rnd and work 2x2 Rib until collar measures approx 2".
BO all sts with Jeny's Surprisingly Stretchy Bind Off.

Finishing
Weave in ends, carefully wash, and block to diagram.

Large Horn Cable

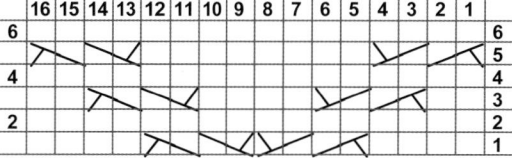

LEGEND

☐ K
RS: Knit stitch
WS: Purl stitch

• P
RS: Purl stitch
WS: Knit stitch

Cable 2 Over 2 Right (2/2 RC)
Sl2 to CN, hold in back; K2, K2 from CN

Cable 2 Over 2 Left (2/2 LC)
Sl2 to CN, hold in front; K2, K2 from CN

Yoke Diamonds

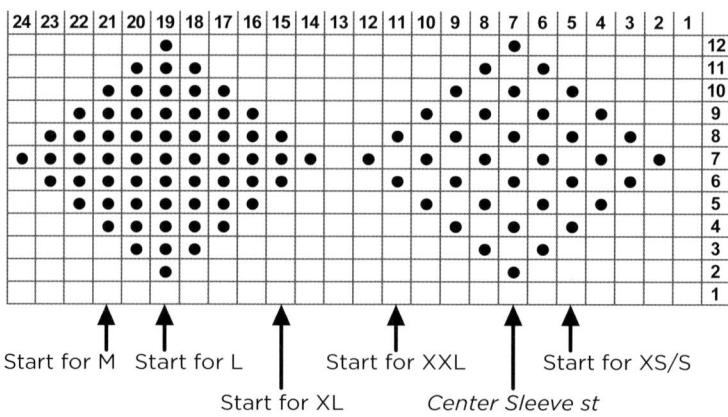

Sleeve Diamonds

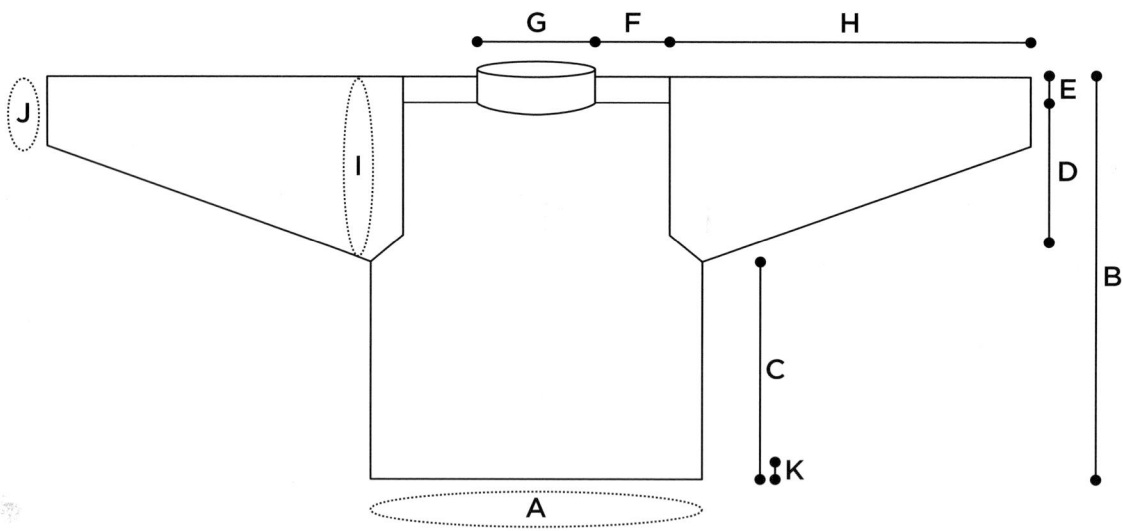

- A 32 (34, 38, 42, 46, 50)"
- B 22 (22.5, 23.25, 24.75, 26, 26.75)"
- C 11.75 (12.5, 12.5, 12.75, 13.25, 13.25)"
- D 7.25 (7.25, 8, 8.5, 9.25, 9.75)" (yoke length after gusset)
- E 1.5 (1.5, 1.5, 1.75, 1.75, 1.75)" (saddle height)
- F 3.75 (3.75, 4.25, 5, 5.75, 6.5)"
- G 5.75 (6, 6.75, 6.76, 6.75, 6.75)"
- H 21 (20.5, 20.5, 20.5, 20.5, 20.5)"
- I 16.75 (16.75, 18.25, 19.5, 20.75, 22.25)"
- J 8 (8, 8, 8, 8.5, 8.5)"
- K 1 (1, 1, 1.25, 1.25, 1.25)" (hem)

OLYMPIC PULLOVER

by Allison Griffith

FINISHED MEASUREMENTS
31 (33.75, 39.75, 43.5, 49.25, 52.25, 55.25, 61.75, 64.75, 67.75)" finished chest circumference; meant to be worn with at least 4" positive ease

YARN
Knit Picks Simply Wool™ (worsted weight, 100% Eco Wool; 218 yards/100g): Winkle 27473, 6 (6, 6, 7, 7, 7, 8, 8, 9, 9) hanks

NEEDLES
US 8 (5mm) straight or circular needles (24" or longer), or size to obtain gauge
US 7 (4.5mm) straight or circular needles (24" or longer), and 16" circular or DPNs, or one size smaller than size used to obtain gauge

NOTIONS
Yarn Needle
Stitch Markers
Cable Needle
Scrap Yarn or Stitch Holder

GAUGE
17 sts and 26 rows = 4" in Stockinette Stitch, blocked
One repeat of Cable Chart, blocked = 2.75" wide x 1.25" tall

For pattern support, contact knittingontheneedles@gmail.com

Olympic Pullover

Notes:
The Olympic Pullover is the classic unisex gansey sweater that's been missing from your everyday wardrobe. Its lushly cabled yoke adds interest and cozy warmth, while basic stockinette makes this sweater simple enough for everyday wear. Traditional dropped shoulders and generously sized arms make this sweater comfy and practical. Worked in Simply Wool Worsted, the Olympic Pullover will stand the test of time, becoming that favorite sweater, an heirloom that you reach for again and again.

The Olympic Pullover is knit flat in pieces, then seamed. The front and back are worked flat from the top down, then seamed at the shoulders. Stitches are picked up around the crew neck and worked in the round for the collar. Then sleeves are worked flat, from the shoulders down. The sleeves are sewn in place at the shoulders, and then the sides and underarms are seamed.

Charts are worked flat; read RS rows (odd numbers) from right to left, and WS rows (even numbers) from left to right.

DIRECTIONS

Back
With larger needles, CO 86 (94, 110, 120, 136, 144, 152, 170, 178, 186) sts.
Setup Row (WS): P6 (10, 3, 8, 1, 5, 9, 3, 7, 11), K1, *P12, K1, P1, K1; rep from * 3 (3, 5, 5, 7, 7, 7, 9, 9, 9) more times, P12, K1, P6 (10, 3, 8, 1, 5, 9, 3, 7, 11).
Row 1 (RS): K6 (10, 3, 8, 1, 5, 9, 3, 7, 11), P1, *work Chart A, work Chart B; rep from * 1 (1, 2, 2, 3, 3, 3, 4, 4, 4) more times, work Sts 1-12 of Chart A, P1, K6 (10, 3, 8, 1, 5, 9, 3, 7, 11).
Row 2 (WS): P6 (10, 3, 8, 1, 5, 9, 3, 7, 11), K1, work Sts 12-1 of Chart A, *work Chart B, work Chart A; rep from * 1 (1, 2, 2, 3, 3, 3, 4, 4, 4) more times, K1, P6 (10, 3, 8, 1, 5, 9, 3, 7, 11).
Work in pattern as established until you've worked Rows 1-12 of charts 6 (6, 7, 7, 8, 8, 8, 9, 9) times, ending with Row 12 (WS row).
Work Rows 1-11 of charts once more.
Dec Row (WS): K7 (11, 4, 9, 2, 6, 10, 4, 8, 12), *K1, K2tog, K1, SSK, K2tog, K1, SSK, K4; rep from * 3 (3, 5, 5, 7, 7, 7, 9, 9, 9) more times, K1, K2tog, K1, SSK, K2tog, K1, SSK, K8 (12, 5, 10, 3, 7, 11, 5, 9, 13). 66 (74, 82, 92, 100, 108, 116, 126, 134, 142) sts.
Knit two rows.
Work St st until Back measures 24 (24, 25, 25, 26, 26, 27, 28, 29, 29)" from CO edge, or 3" shorter than desired length.
On next RS row, switch to smaller needles and K across, decreasing 0 (0, 0, 2, 2, 2, 2, 0, 0, 0) sts evenly. 66 (74, 82, 90, 98, 106, 114, 126, 134, 142) sts.
Work 2x2 Rib for 3", or desired length.
BO loosely in pattern. Set aside.

Front
Shoulders are worked separately, then joined at bottom of neck; body is then worked in a single piece to hem.
Left Shoulder
With larger needles, CO 24 (27, 35, 38, 45, 47, 50, 58, 61, 64) sts.
Setup Row (WS): P6 (10, 3, 8, 1, 5, 9, 3, 7, 11), K1, *P12, K1, P1, K1; rep from * 0 (0, 1, 0, 1, 1, 1, 2, 2, 2) more time(s), P0 (0, 0, 12, 12, 6, 6, 6, 6, 6), PM, P2 (1, 1, 2, 1, 5, 4, 3, 2, 1).

Size 31" Only
Row 1 (RS): K to M, SM, P1, K1, P1, work Sts 1-12 of Chart B, P1, K6.
Row 2 (WS): P6, K1, work Sts 12-1 of Chart B, K1, P1, K1, SM, P to end.

Size 33.75" Only
Row 1 (RS): K to M, SM, P1, K1, P1, work Sts 1-12 of Chart B, P1, K10.
Row 2 (WS): P10, K1, work Sts 12-1 of Chart B, K1, P1, K1, SM, P to end.

Size 39.75" Only
Row 1 (RS): K to M, SM, P1, K1, P1, work Chart A, work Sts 1-12 of Chart B, P1, K3.
Row 2 (WS): P3, K1, work Sts 12-1 of Chart B, work Chart A, K1, P1, K1, SM, P to end.

Size 43.5" Only
Row 1 (RS): K to M, SM, work Chart A, work Sts 1-12 of Chart B, P1, K8.
Row 2 (WS): P8, K1, work Sts 12-1 of Chart B, work Chart A, SM, P to end.

Size 49.25" Only
Row 1 (RS): K to M, SM, work Chart B, work Chart A, work Sts 1-12 of Chart B, P1, K1.
Row 2 (WS): P1, K1, work Sts 12-1 of Chart B, work Chart A, work Chart B, SM, P to end.

Size 52.25" Only
Row 1 (RS): K to M, SM, work Sts 7-15 Chart B, work Chart A, work Sts 1-12 of Chart B, P1, K5.
Row 2 (WS): P5, K1, work Sts 12-1 of Chart B, work Chart A, work sts 15-7 of Chart B, SM, P to end

Size 55.25" Only
Row 1 (RS): K to M, SM, work Sts 7-15 Chart B, work Chart A, work Sts 1-12 of Chart B, P1, K9.
Row 2 (WS): P9, K1, work Sts 12-1 of Chart B, work Chart A, work sts 15-7 of Chart B, SM, P to end.

Size 61.75" Only
Row 1 (RS): K to M, SM, work Sts 7-15 of Chart A, work Chart B, work Chart A, work Sts 1-12 of Chart B, P1, K3.
Row 2 (WS): P3, K1, work Sts 12-1 of Chart B, work Chart A, work Chart B, work sts 15-7 of Chart A, SM, P to end.

Size 64.75" Only
Row 1 (RS): K to M, SM, work Sts 7-15 of Chart A, work Chart B, work Chart A, work Sts 1-12 of Chart B, P1, K7.
Row 2 (WS): P7, K1, work Sts 12-1 of Chart B, work Chart A, work Chart B, work Sts 15-7 of Chart A, SM, P to end.

Size 67.75" Only
Row 1 (RS): K to M, SM, work Sts 7-15 of Chart A, work Chart B, work Chart A, work Sts 1-12 of Chart B, P1, K11.
Row 2 (WS): P11, K1, work Sts 12-1 of Chart B, work Chart A, work Chart B, work Sts 15-7 of Chart A, SM, P to end.

All Sizes Resume
Rep Rows 1-2 until you've worked Chart Rows 1-12 once, ending with Row 12.

Begin Neck Shaping
Row 1 and all odd-numbered rows (RS): K to M, work in pattern to end.
Row 2 (WS): Work in pattern to 1 st before end, M1, P1. 1 st inc. 25 (28, 36, 39, 46, 48, 51, 59, 62, 65) sts.
Row 4: Rep Row 2. 1 st inc. 26 (29, 37, 40, 47, 49, 52, 60, 63, 66) sts.
Row 6: Work in pattern to end, CO 3 sts using Backward Loop Cast On. 29 (32, 40, 43, 50, 52, 55, 63, 66, 69) sts.
Row 8: Work in pattern to end, CO 4 sts using Backward Loop Cast On. 33 (36, 44, 47, 54, 56, 59, 67, 70, 73) sts. Transfer sts to scrap yarn or st holder and set aside.

Right Shoulder
With larger needles, CO 24 (27, 35, 38, 45, 47, 50, 58, 61, 64) sts.
Setup Row (WS): P2 (1, 1, 2, 1, 5, 4, 3, 2, 1), PM, P0 (0, 0, 12, 12, 6, 6, 6, 6, 6), *K1, P1, K1, P12; rep from * 0 (0, 1, 0, 1, 1, 1, 2, 2, 2) more time(s), K1, P6 (10, 3, 8, 1, 5, 9, 3, 7, 11).

Size 31" Only
Row 1 (RS): K6, P1, work Chart B, SM, K to end.
Row 2 (WS): P to M, SM, work Chart B, K1, P6.

Size 33.75" Only
Row 1 (RS): K10, P1, work Chart B, SM, K to end.
Row 2 (WS): P to M, SM, work Chart B, K1, P10.

Size 39.75" Only
Row 1 (RS): K3, P1, work Chart B, work Chart A, SM, K to end.
Row 2 (WS): P to M, SM, work Chart A, work Chart B, K1, P3.

Size 43.5" Only
Row 1 (RS): K8, P1, work Chart B, work Sts 1-12 of Chart A, SM, K to end.
Row 2 (WS): P to M, SM, work Sts 12-1 of Chart A, work Chart B, K1, P8.

Size 49.25" Only
Row 1 (RS): K1, P1, work Chart B, work Chart A, work Sts 1-12 of Chart B, SM, K to end.
Row 2 (WS): P to M, SM, work Sts 12-1 of Chart B, work Chart A, Chart B, K1, P1.

Size 52.25" Only
Row 1 (RS): K5, P1, work Chart B, work Chart A, work Sts 1-6 of Chart B, SM, K to end.
Row 2 (WS): P to M, SM, work Sts 6-1 of Chart B, work Chart A, Chart B, K1, P5.

Size 54.5" Only
Row 1 (RS): K9, P1, work Chart B, work Chart A, work Sts 1-6 of Chart B, SM, K to end.
Row 2 (WS): P to M, SM, work Sts 6-1 of Chart B, work Chart A, work Chart B, K1, P9.

Size 61.75" Only
Row 1 (RS): K3, P1, work Chart B, work Chart A, work Chart B, work Sts 1-6 of Chart A, SM, K to end.
Row 2 (WS): P to M, SM, work Sts 6-1 of Chart A, work Chart B, work Chart A, work Chart B, K1, P3.

Size 64.75" Only
Row 1 (RS): K7, P1, work Chart B, work Chart A, work Chart B, work Sts 1-6 of Chart A, SM, K to end.
Row 2 (WS): P to M, SM, work Sts 6-1 of Chart A, work Chart B, work Chart A, work Chart B, K1, P7.

Size 67.75" Only
Row 1 (RS): K11, P1, work Chart B, work Chart A, work Chart B, work Sts 1-6 of Chart A, SM, K to end.
Row 2 (WS): P to M, SM, work Sts 6-1 of Chart A, work Chart B, work Chart A, work Chart B, K1, P11.

All Sizes Resume
Rep Rows 1-2 until you've worked Chart Rows 1-12 once, ending with Row 12.

Begin Neck Shaping
Row 1 (RS): Work in pattern to 1 st before end, M1, K1. 1 st inc. 25 (28, 36, 39, 46, 48, 51, 59, 62, 65) sts.
Row 2 and all even-numbered rows (WS): P to M, work in pattern to end.
Row 3: Rep Row 1. 1 st inc. 26 (29, 37, 40, 47, 49, 52, 60, 63, 66) sts.
Row 5: Work in pattern to end, CO 3 sts using Backward Loop Cast On. 29 (32, 40, 43, 50, 52, 55, 63, 66, 69) sts.
Row 7: Work in pattern to end, CO 4 sts using Backward Loop Cast On. 33 (36, 44, 47, 54, 56, 59, 67, 70, 73) sts.
Row 8: P to M, work in pattern to end.

Join Shoulders
Next Row (RS): Work in pattern across Right Shoulder to M, remove M, K to end, CO 20 (22, 22, 26, 28, 32, 34, 36, 38, 40) sts using Backward Loop Cast On, K across Left Shoulder to M, remove M, work in pattern to end. 86 (94, 110, 120, 136, 144, 152, 170, 178, 186) sts.
Setup Row (WS): P6 (10, 3, 8, 1, 5, 9, 3, 7, 11), K1, *P12, K1, P1, K1; rep from * 3 (3, 5, 5, 7, 7, 7, 9, 9, 9) more times, P12, K1, P6 (10, 3, 8, 1, 5, 9, 3, 7, 11).
Row 1 (RS): K6 (10, 3, 8, 1, 5, 9, 3, 7, 11), P1, *work Chart B, work Chart A; rep from * 1 (1, 2, 2, 3, 3, 3, 4, 4, 4) more times, work Sts 1-12 of Chart B, P1, K6 (10, 3, 8, 1, 5, 9, 3, 7, 11).
Row 2 (WS): P6 (10, 3, 8, 1, 5, 9, 3, 7, 11), K1, work Sts 12-1 of Chart B, *work Chart A, work Chart B; rep from * 1 (1, 2, 2, 3, 3, 3, 4, 4, 4) more times, K1, P6 (10, 3, 8, 1, 5, 9, 3, 7, 11).

Rep Rows 1-2 until you've worked Chart Rows 1-12 6 (6, 7, 7, 7, 8, 8, 8, 9, 9) times (including reps worked on shoulders), ending with Row 12 (WS row).

Work Chart Rows 1-11 once more.

Dec Row (WS): K7 (11, 4, 9, 2, 6, 10, 4, 8, 12), *K1, K2tog, K1, SSK, K2tog, K1, SSK, K4; rep from * 3 (3, 5, 5, 7, 7, 7, 9, 9, 9) more times, K1, K2tog, K1, SSK, K2tog, K1, SSK, K8 (12, 5, 10, 3, 7, 11, 5, 9, 13). 66 (74, 82, 92, 100, 108, 116, 126, 134, 142) sts. Knit two rows.

Work St st until Front measures 24 (24, 25, 25, 26, 26, 27, 28, 29, 29)" from top of shoulder, or 3" shorter than desired length.

On next RS row, switch to smaller needles and K across, decreasing 0 (0, 0, 2, 2, 2, 2, 0, 0, 0) sts evenly. 66 (74, 82, 90, 98, 106, 114, 126, 134, 142) sts.

Work 2x2 Rib for 3", or desired length.

BO loosely in pattern.

Sew Front and Back together at shoulders, matching cables as closely as possible.

Collar

With smaller 16" circular needles, PU and K 92 (96, 100, 104, 112, 120, 124, 128, 132, 136) sts around neck, beginning at center back. PM and prepare to work in the rnd.

Work 2x2 Rib until collar measures 1" from picked up edge.

BO loosely in pattern. Set aside.

Sleeves (make two the same)

With larger needles, CO 68 (72, 76, 80, 84, 90, 94, 98, 102, 106) sts.

Work flat in St st for 15 (7, 7, 17, 17, 5, 5, 23, 15, 11) rows, starting with a WS row.

*Work St st for 5 (5, 5, 4, 4, 4, 3, 3, 3) rows, then work the appropriate Dec Row.

RS Dec Row: K1, SSK, K to 3 sts before end, K2tog, K. 2 sts dec.

WS Dec Row: P1, SSP, P to 3 sts before end, P2tog, P. 2 sts dec.

Rep from * until you've worked 15 (17, 17, 19, 19, 22, 22, 24, 26, 28) total Dec Rows. 38 (38, 42, 42, 46, 46, 50, 50, 50, 50) sts.

Work St st without shaping until sleeve measures 16.5 (17, 17, 17.5, 17.5, 18, 18, 18.5, 18.5, 19)" from CO edge or 3" shorter than desired.

On next RS row, switch to smaller needles and K across.

Work 2x2 Rib for 3" or desired length.

BO loosely in pattern.

Finishing

Wash and block pieces separately if you prefer.

Sew CO edge of sleeves to shoulders, centering sleeve at shoulder seam, and distributing sleeve evenly on either side before sewing in place. Sew sleeve/side seams, matching cuffs, hems, and underarm seams.

Weave in ends, wash, and block to diagram if you have not already blocked before seaming.

A 31 (33.75, 39.75, 43.5, 49.25, 52.25, 55.25, 61.75, 64.75, 67.75)"

B 27 (27, 28, 28, 29, 29, 30, 31, 32, 32)"

C 19.5 (20, 20, 20.5, 20.5, 21, 21, 21.5, 21.5, 22)"

D 15.75 (16.75, 17.75, 18.5, 19.5, 21, 22, 22.75, 23.75, 24.75)"

E 8.75 (8.75, 9.75, 9.75, 10.5, 10.5, 11.5, 11.5, 11.5, 11.5)"

F 3.25"

G 21.75 (22.5, 23.5, 24.5, 26.25, 28.25, 29.25, 30, 31, 32)"

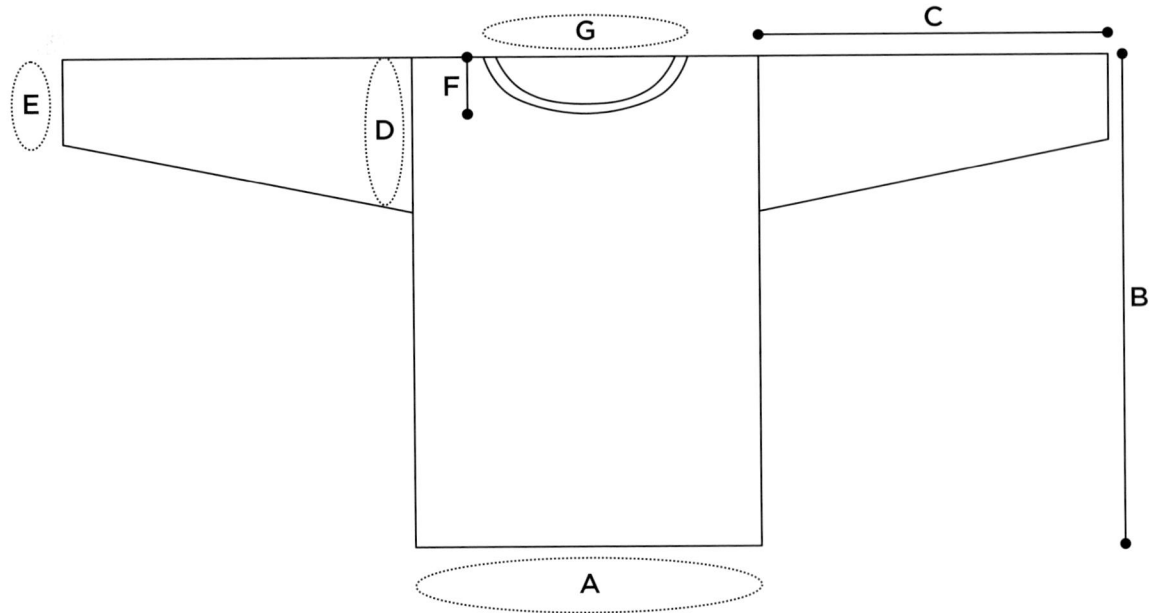

LEGEND

☐ **K**
RS: Knit stitch
WS: Purl stitch

⬤ **P**
RS: Purl stitch
WS: Knit stitch

Cable 3 Over 3 Right (3/3 RC)
Sl3 to CN, hold in back; K3, K3 from CN

Cable 3 Over 3 Left (3/3 LC)
Sl3 to CN, hold in front; K3, K3 from CN

Cable 3 Over 3 Right, Purl back (3/3 RPC)
Sl3 to CN, hold in back; K3, P3 from CN

Cable 3 Over 3 Left, Purl back (3/3 LPC)
Sl3 to CN, hold in front; P3, K3 from CN

Olympic Chart A

Olympic Chart B

PLEINMONT

by Bridget Pupillo

FINISHED MEASUREMENTS
32 (36, 40, 44, 48, 52)" finished chest circumference; meant to be worn with 0-4" positive ease

YARN
Knit Picks Simply Wool™ (bulky weight, 100% Eco Wool; 193 yards/100g): Winnie 27478, 5 (6, 7, 8, 9, 10) hanks

NEEDLES
US 9 (5.5mm) 16" and 32" circular needles and DPNs, or size to obtain gauge
US 8 (5mm) 16" and 32" circular needles and DPNs, or one size smaller than size used to obtain gauge

NOTIONS
Yarn Needle
Stitch Markers
Cable Needle or Extra DPN
Scrap Yarn or Stitch Holders

GAUGE
16 sts and 20 rnds = 4" in Stockinette Stitch in the round on larger needles, blocked
20 sts and 24 rnds = 4" in Cable Pattern on larger needles, blocked

For pattern support, contact brigittissima@gmail.com

Pleinmont

Notes:

Pleinmont combines traditional guernsey construction and motifs with an all-over cable design and bulkier weight yarn for a fresh, gender-neutral look. The design and construction are simple, and the bulky yarn knits up quickly, making this an ideal choice for a first-time guernsey project.

The Pleinmont guernsey is worked in the round from the bottom up to the underarms. The Back and Front are worked flat and separately, then sewn together at the shoulder seams. The sleeves are worked separately in the round and sewn to the body. The ribbed neck is picked up and worked in the round after all pieces are sewn together.

Stitch patterns are written and charted. The body charts (Chart 1) are worked flat; read RS rows (odd numbers) from right to left, and WS rows (even numbers) from left to right. The sleeve chart (Chart 2) is worked in the round; read each chart row from right to left as a RS row. Written instructions for each chart reflect these differences and should be worked as written.

Reverse Stockinette Stitch (Rev St st, flat over any number of sts)
Row 1 (RS): P across.
Row 2 (WS): K across.
Rep Rows 1-2 for pattern.

Reverse Stockinette Stitch (Rev St st, in the round over any number of sts)
All Rnds: P all.

Cable 2 Over 2 Left (2/2 LC)
Sl2 to CN, hold in front; K2, K2 from CN.

Cable 2 Over 2 Right (2/2 RC)
Sl2 to CN, hold in back; K2, K2 from CN.

Cable 2 Over 1 Left, Purl back (2/1 LPC)
Sl2 to CN, hold in front; P1, K2 from CN.

Cable 2 Over 1 Right, Purl back (2/1 RPC)
Sl1 to CN, hold in back; K2, P1 from CN.

Chart 1—Size 32" (flat over 74 sts)
Row 1 (RS): K1, P8, K2, P4, K2, P8, K2, P6, K8, P6, K2, P8, K2, P4, K2, P8, K1.
Row 2 (WS): P2, K7, P2, K4, P2, K8, P2, K5, P10, K5, P2, K8, P2, K4, P2, K7, P2.
Row 3: K3, P6, 2/2 LC, 2/2 RC, P8, 2/2 LC, P2, K5, P2, K5, P2, 2/2 RC, P8, 2/2 LC, 2/2 RC, P6, K3.
Row 4: P3, K6, P8, K8, P4, K2, P4, K4, P4, K2, P4, K8, P8, K6, P3.
Row 5: K3, P6, K8, P8, K4, P2, K3, P2, K2, P2, K3, P2, K4, P8, K8, P6, K3.
Row 6: K1, P2, K6, P8, K8, P4, K2, P2, K2, P4, K2, P2, K2, P4, K8, P8, K6, P2, K1.
Row 7: P2, K1, P6, 2/2 LC, 2/2 RC, P8, 2/2 LC, P2, K1, P2, K6, P2, K1, P2, 2/2 RC, P8, 2/2 RC, P6, K1, P2.
Row 8: P1, K8, P8, K8, P4, K4, P8, K4, P4, K8, P8, K8, P1.
Row 9: K2, P7, K8, P8, K4, P3, K10, P3, K4, P8, K8, P7, K2.
Row 10: P3, K6, P8, K8, P4, K2, P5, K2, P5, K2, P4, K8, P8, K6, P3.
Row 11: K3, P6, 2/2 LC, 2/2 RC, P8, 2/2 LC, P2, K4, P4, K4, P2, 2/2 RC, P8, 2/2 LC, 2/2 RC, P6, K3.
Row 12: P3, K6, P8, K8, P4, K2, P3, K2, P2, K2, P3, K2, P4, K8, P8, K6, P3
Row 13: P1, K2, P5, 2/1 RPC, P4, 2/1 LPC, P6, 2/1 RPC, P4, K2, P2, K4, P2, K2, P4, 2/1 LPC, P6, 2/1 RPC, P4, 2/1 LPC, P5, K2, P1.
Row 14: K2, P1, K5, P2, K6, P2, K6, P2, K5, P1, K2, P6, K2, P1, K5, P2, K6, P2, K6, P2, K5, P1, K2.
Row 15: K1, P6, 2/1 RPC, P6, 2/1 LPC, P4, 2/1 RPC, P7, K8, P7, 2/1 LPC, P4, 2/1 RPC, P6, 2/1 LPC, P6, K1.
Row 16: P2, K5, P2, K8, P2, K4, P2, K7, P10, K7, P2, K4, P2, K8, P2, K5, P2.
Row 17: K3, P2, 2/2 RC, P8, 2/2 LC, 2/2 RC, P6, K5, P2, K5, P6, 2/2LC, 2/2 RC, P8, 2/2 LC, P2, K3.
Row 18: P3, K2, P4, K8, P8, K6, P4, K4, P4, K6, P8, K8, P4, K2, P3.
Row 19: K3, P2, K4, P8, K8, P6, K3, P2, K2, P2, K3, P6, K8, P8, K4, P2, K3.
Row 20: K1, P2, K2, P4, K8, P8, K6, P2, K2, P4, K2, P2, K6, P8, K8, P4, K2, P2, K1.
Row 21: P2, K1, P2, 2/2 RC, P8, 2/2 LC, 2/2 RC, P6, K1, P2, K6, P2, K1, P6, 2/2 LC, 2/2 RC, P8, 2/2 LC, P2, K1, P2.
Row 22: P1, K4, P4, (K8, P8) three times, K8, P4, K4, P1.
Row 23: K2, P3, K4, P8, K8, P7, K10, P7, K8, P8, K4, P3, K2.
Row 24: P3, K2, P4, K8, P8, K6, P5, K2, P5, K6, P8, K8, P4, K2, P3.
Row 25: K3, P2, 2/2 RC, P8, 2/2 LC, 2/2 RC, P6, K4, P4, K4, P6, 2/2 LC, 2/2 RC, P8, 2/2 LC, P2, K3.
Row 26: P3, K2, P4, K8, P8, K6, P3, K2, P2, K2, P3, K6, P8, K8, P4, K2, P3.
Row 27: P1, K2, P4, 2/1 LPC, P6, 2/1 RPC, P4, 2/1 LPC, P5, K2, P2, K4, P2, K2, P5, 2/1 RPC, P4, 2/1 LPC, P6, 2/1 RPC, P4, K2, P1.
Row 28: K2, P1, K5, (P2, K6) two times, P2, K5, P1, K2, P6, K2, P1, K5, (P2, K6) two times, P2, K5, P1, K2.
Row 29: K1, P7, 2/1 LPC, P4, 2/1 RPC, P6, 2/1 LPC, P6, K8, P6, 2/1 RPC, P6, 2/1 LPC, P4, 2/1 RPC, P7, K1.
Row 30: P2, K7, P2, K4, P2, K8, P2, K5, P10, K5, P2, K8, P2, K4, P2, K7, P2.
After working Rows 1-30, rep Rows 3-30 for pattern.

Chart 1—Size 36" (flat over 82 sts)
Row 1 (RS): K5, P8, K2, P4, K2, P8, K2, P6, K8, P6, K2, P8, K2, P4, K2, P8, K5.
Row 2 (WS): P6, K7, P2, K4, P2, K8, P2, K5, P10, K5, P2, K8, P2, K4, P2, K7, P6.
Row 3: K1, P1, K5, P6, 2/2 LC, 2/2 RC, P8, 2/2 LC, P2, K5, P2, K5, P2, 2/2 RC, P8, 2/2 LC, 2/2 RC, P6, K5, P1, K1.
Row 4: P1, K2, P4, K6, P8, K8, P4, K2, P4, K4, P4, K2, P4, K8, P8, K6, P4, K2, P1.

Row 5: K2, P2, K3, P6, K8, P8, K4, P2, K3, P2, K2, P2, K3, P2, K4, P8, K8, P6, K3, P2, K2.
Row 6: P3, K2, P2, K6, P8, K8, P4, K2, P2, K2, P4, P2, K2, P4, K8, P8, K6, P2, K2, P3.
Row 7: K4, P2, K1, P6, 2/2 LC, 2/2 RC, P8, 2/2 LC, P2, K1, P2, K6, P2, K1, P2, 2/2 RC, P8, 2/2 LC, 2/2 RC, P6, K1, P2, K4.
Row 8: P5, K8, P8, K8, P4, K4, P8, K4, P4, K8, P8, K8, P5.
Row 9: K6, P7, K8, P8, K4, P3, K10, P3, K4, P8, K8, P7, K6.
Row 10: P1, K1, P5, K6, P8, K8, P4, K2, P5, K2, P5, K2, P4, K8, P8, K6, P5, K1, P1.
Row 11: K1, P2, K4, P6, 2/2 LC, 2/2 RC, P8, 2/2 LC, P2, K4, P4, K4, P2, 2/2 RC, P8, 2/2 LC, 2/2 RC, P6, K4, P2, K1.
Row 12: P2, K2, P3, K6, P8, K8, P4, K2, P3, K2, P2, K2, P3, K2, P4, K8, P8, K6, P3, K2, P2.
Row 13: K3, P2, K2, P5, 2/1 RPC, P4, 2/1 LPC, P6, 2/1 RPC, P4, K2, P2, K4, P2, K2, P4, 2/1 LPC, P6, 2/1 RPC, P4, 2/1 LPC, P5, K2, P2, K3.
Row 14: P4, K2, P1, K5, P2, K6, P2, K6, P2, K5, P1, K2, P6, K2, P1, K5, P2, K6, P2, K6, P2, K5, P1, K2, P4.
Row 15: K5, P6, 2/1 RPC, P6, 2/1 LPC, P4, 2/1 RPC, P7, K8, P7, 2/1 LPC, P4, 2/1 RPC, P6, 2/1 LPC, P6, K5.
Row 16: P6, K5, P2, K8, P2, K4, P2, K7, P10, K7, P2, K4, P2, K8, P2, K5, P6.
Row 17: K1, P1, K5, P2, 2/2 RC, P8, 2/2 LC, 2/2 RC, P6, K5, P2, K5, P6, 2/2 LC, 2/2 RC, P8, 2/2 LC, P2, K5, P1, K1.
Row 18: P1, K2, P4, K2, P4, K8, P8, K6, P4, K4, P4, K6, P8, K8, P4, K2, P4, K2, P1.
Row 19: K2, P2, K3, P2, K4, P8, K8, P6, K3, P2, K2, P2, K3, P6, K8, P8, K4, P2, K3, P2, K2.
Row 20: P3, K2, P2, K2, P4, K8, P8, K6, P2, K2, P4, K2, P2, K6, P8, K8, P4, K2, P2, K2, P3.
Row 21: K4, P2, K1, P2, 2/2 RC, P8, 2/2 LC, 2/2 RC, P6, K1, P2, K6, P2, K1, P6, 2/2 LC, 2/2 RC, P8, 2/2 LC, P2, K1, P2, K4.
Row 22: P5, K4, P4, (K8, P8) three times, K8, P4, K4, P5.
Row 23: K6, P3, K4, P8, K8, P7, K10, P7, K8, P8, K4, P3, K6.
Row 24: P1, K1, P5, K2, P4, K8, P8, K6, P5, K2, P5, K6, P8, K8, P4, K2, P5, K1, P1.
Row 25: K1, P2, K4, P2, 2/2 RC, P8, 2/2 LC, 2/2 RC, P6, K4, P4, K4, P6, 2/2 LC, 2/2 RC, P8, 2/2 LC, P2, K4, P2, K1.
Row 26: P2, K2, P3, K2, P4, K8, P8, K6, P3, K2, P2, K2, P3, K6, P8, K8, P4, K2, P3, K2, P2.
Row 27: K3, P2, K2, P4, 2/1 LPC, P6, 2/1 RPC, P4, 2/1 LPC, P5, K2, P2, K4, P2, K2, P5, 2/1 RPC, P4, 2/1 LPC, P6, 2/1 RPC, P4, K2, P2, K3.
Row 28: P4, K2, P1, K5, (P2, K6) two times, P2, K5, P1, K2, P6, K2, P1, K5, (P2, K6) two times, P2, K5, P1, K2, P4.
Row 29: K5, P7, 2/1 LPC, P4, 2/1 RPC, P6, 2/1 LPC, P6, K8, P6, 2/1 RPC, P6, 2/1 LPC, P4, 2/1 RPC, P7, K5.
Row 30: P6, K7, P2, K4, P2, K8, P2, K5, P10, K5, P2, K8, P2, K4, P2, K7, P6.

After working Rows 1-30, rep Rows 3-30 for pattern.

Chart 1—Size 40″ (flat over 92 sts)
Row 1 (RS): K2, P6, K2, P8, K2, P4, K2, P8, K2, P6, K8, P6, K2, P8, K2, P4, K2, P8, K2, P6, K2.
Row 2 (WS): P3, K5, P2, K8, P2, K4, P2, K8, P2, K5, P10, K5, P2, K8, P2, K4, P2, K8, P2, K5, P3.
Row 3: K4, P2, 2/2 RC, P8, 2/2 LC, 2/2 RC, P8, 2/2 LC, P2, K5, P2, K5, P2, 2/2 RC, P8, 2/2 LC, 2/2 RC, P8, 2/2 LC, P2, K4.
Row 4: P4, K2, P4, K8, P8, K8, P4, K2, P4, K4, P4, K2, P4, K8, P8, K8, P4, K2, P4.
Row 5: P1, K3, P2, K4, P8, K8, P4, K2, P4, P2, K2, P2, K3, P2, K4, P8, K8, P8, K4, P2, K3, P1.
Row 6: K2, P2, K2, P4, K8, P8, K8, P4, K2, P2, K2, P4, K2, P2, K2, P4, K8, P8, K8, P4, K2, P2, K2.
Row 7: K1, P2, K1, P2, 2/2 RC, P8, 2/2 LC, 2/2 RC, P8, 2/2 LC, P2, K1, P2, K6, P2, K1, P2, 2/2 RC, P8, 2/2 LC, 2/2 RC, P8, 2/2 LC, P2, K1, P2, K1.
Row 8: P2, K4, P4, K8, P8, K8, P4, K4, P8, K4, P4, K8, P8, K8, P4, K4, P2.
Row 9: K3, P3, K4, P8, K8, P8, K4, P3, K10, P3, K4, P8, K8, P8, K4, P3, K3.
Row 10: P4, K2, P4, K8, P8, K8, P4, K2, P5, K2, P5, K2, P4, K8, P8, K8, P4, K2, P4.
Row 11: K4, P2, 2/2 RC, P8, 2/2 LC, 2/2 RC, P8, 2/2 LC, P2, K4, P4, K4, P2, 2/2 RC, P8, 2/2 LC, 2/2 RC, P8, 2/2 LC, P2, K4.
Row 12: K1, P3, K2, P4, K8, P8, K8, P4, K2, P3, K2, P2, K2, P3, K2, P4, K8, P8, K8, P4, K2, P3, K1.
Row 13: P2, K2, P4, 2/1 LPC, P6, 2/1 RPC, P4, 2/1 LPC, P6, 2/1 RPC, P4, K2, P2, K4, P2, K2, P4, 2/1 LPC, P6, 2/1 RPC, P4, 2/1 LPC, P6, 2/1 RPC, P4, K2, P2.
Row 14: P1, K2, P1, K5, P2, K6, P2, K6, P2, K5, P1, K2, P6, K2, P1, K5, P2, K6, P2, K6, P2, K5, P1, K2, P1.
Row 15: K2, P7, 2/1 LPC, P4, 2/1 RPC, P6, 2/1 LPC, P4, 2/1 RPC, P7, K8, P7, 2/1 LPC, P4, 2/1 RPC, P6, 2/1 LPC, P4, 2/1 RPC, P7, K2.
Row 16: P3, K7, P2, K4, P2, K8, P2, K4, P2, K7, P10, K7, P2, K4, P2, K8, P2, K4, P2, K7, P3.
Row 17: K4, P6, 2/2 LC, 2/2 RC, P8, 2/2 LC, 2/2 RC, P6, K5, P2, K5, P6, 2/2 LC, 2/2 RC, P8, 2/2 LC, 2/2 RC, P6, K4.
Row 18: P4, K6, P8, K8, P8, K6, P4, K4, P4, K6, P8, K8, P8, K6, P4.
Row 19: P1, K3, P6, K8, P8, K8, P6, K3, P2, K2, P2, K3, P6, K8, P8, K8, P6, K3, P1.
Row 20: K2, P2, K6, P8, K8, P8, K6, P2, K2, P4, K2, P2, K6, P8, K8, P8, K6, P2, K2.
Row 21: K1, P2, K1, P6, 2/2 LC, 2/2 RC, P8, 2/2 LC, 2/2 RC, P6, K1, P2, K6, P2, K1, P6, 2/2 LC, 2/2 RC, P8, 2/2 LC, 2/2 RC, P6, K1, P2, K1.
Row 22: P2, (K8, P8) five times, K8, P2.
Row 23: K3, P7, K8, P8, K8, P7, K10, P7, K8, P8, K8, P7, K3.
Row 24: P4, K6, P8, K8, P8, K6, P5, K2, P5, K6, P8, K8, P8, K6, P4.
Row 25: K4, P6, 2/2 LC, 2/2 RC, P8, 2/2 LC, 2/2 RC, P6, K4, P4, K4, P6, 2/2 LC, 2/2 RC, P8, 2/2 LC, 2/2 RC, P6, K4.
Row 26: K1, P3, K6, P8, K8, P8, K6, P3, K2, P2, K2, P3, K6, P8, K8, P8, K6, P3, K1.
Row 27: P2, K2, P5, 2/1 RPC, P4, 2/1 LPC, P6, 2/1 RPC, P4, 2/1 LPC, P5, K2, P2, K4, P2, K2, P5, 2/1 RPC, P4, 2/1 LPC, P6, 2/1 RPC, P4, 2/1 LPC, P5, K2, P2.
Row 28: P1, K2, P1, K5, (P2, K6) three times, P2, K5, P1, K2, P6, K2, P1, K5, (P2, K6) three times, P2, K5, P1, K2, P1.

Row 29: K2, P6, 2/1 RPC, P6, 2/1 LPC, P4, 2/1 RPC, P6, 2/1 LPC, P6, K8, P6, 2/1 RPC, P6, 2/1 LPC, P4, 2/1 RPC, P6, 2/1 LPC, P6, K2.
Row 30: P3, K5, P2, K8, P2, K4, P2, K8, P2, K5, P10, K5, P2, K8, P2, K4, P2, K8, P2, K5, P3.
After working Rows 1-30, rep Rows 3-30 for pattern.

Chart 1—Size 44" (flat over 100 sts)
Row 1 (RS): K6, P6, K2, P8, K2, P4, K2, P8, K2, P6, K8, P6, K2, P8, K2, P4, K2, P8, K2, P6, K6.
Row 2 (WS): P7, K5, P2, K8, P2, K4, P2, K8, P2, K5, P10, K5, P2, K8, P2, K4, P2, K8, P2, K5, P7.
Row 3: K2, P1, K5, P2, 2/2 RC, P8, 2/2 LC, P2, 2/2 RC, P8, 2/2 LC, P2, K5, P2, K5, P2, 2/2 RC, P8, 2/2 LC, P2, 2/2 RC, P8, 2/2 LC, P2, K5, P1, K2.
Row 4: P2, K2, P4, K2, P4, K8, P8, K8, P4, K2, P4, K4, P4, K2, P4, K8, P8, K8, P4, K2, P4, K2, P2.
Row 5: K3, P2, K3, P2, K4, P8, K8, P8, K4, P2, K3, P2, K2, P2, K3, P2, K4, P8, K8, P8, K4, P2, K3, P2, K3.
Row 6: P4, K2, P2, K2, P4, K8, P8, K8, P4, K2, P2, K2, P4, K2, P2, K2, P4, K8, P8, K8, P4, K2, P2, K2, P4.
Row 7: K5, P2, K1, P2, 2/2 RC, P8, 2/2 LC, 2/2 RC, P8, 2/2 LC, P2, K1, P2, K6, P2, K1, P2, 2/2 RC, P8, 2/2 LC, 2/2 RC, P8, 2/2 LC, P2, K1, P2, K5.
Row 8: P6, K4, P4, K8, P8, K8, P4, K4, P8, K4, P4, K8, P8, K8, P4, K4, P6.
Row 9: K7, P3, K4, P8, K8, P8, K4, P3, K10, P3, K4, P8, K8, P8, K4, P3, K7.
Row 10: P2, K1, P5, K2, P4, K8, P8, K8, P4, K2, P5, K2, P5, K2, P4, K8, P8, K8, P4, K2, P5, K1, P2.
Row 11: K2, P2, K4, P2, 2/2 RC, P8, 2/2 LC, 2/2 RC, P8, 2/2 LC, P2, K4, P4, K4, P2, 2/2 RC, P8, 2/2 LC, 2/2 RC, P8, 2/2 LC, P2, K4, P2, K2.
Row 12: P3, K2, P3, K2, P4, K8, P8, K8, P4, K2, P3, K2, P2, K2, P3, K2, P4, K8, P8, K8, P4, K2, P3, K2, P3.
Row 13: K4, P2, K2, P4, 2/1 LPC, P6, 2/1 RPC, P4, 2/1 LPC, P6, 2/1 RPC, P4, K2, P2, K4, P2, K2, P4, 2/1 LPC, P6, 2/1 RPC, P4, 2/1 LPC, P6, 2/1 RPC, P4, K2, P2, K4.
Row 14: P5, K2, P1, K5, P2, K6, P2, K6, P2, K6, P2, K5, P1, K2, P6, K2, P1, K5, P2, K6, P2, K6, P2, K6, P2, K5, P1, K2, P5.
Row 15: K6, P7, 2/1 LPC, P4, 2/1 RPC, P6, 2/1 LPC, P4, 2/1 RPC, P7, K8, P7, 2/1 LPC, P4, 2/1 RPC, P6, 2/1 LPC, P4, 2/1 RPC, P7, K6.
Row 16: P7, K7, P2, K4, P2, K8, P2, K4, P2, K7, P10, K7, P2, K4, P2, K8, P2, K4, P2, K7, P7.
Row 17: K2, P1, K5, P6, 2/2 LC, 2/2 RC, P8, 2/2 LC, 2/2 RC, P6, K5, P2, K5, P6, 2/2 LC, 2/2 RC, P8, 2/2 LC, 2/2 RC, P6, K5, P1, K2.
Row 18: P2, K2, P4, K6, P8, K8, P8, K6, P4, K4, P4, K6, P8, K8, P8, K6, P4, K2, P2.
Row 19: K3, P2, K3, P6, K8, P8, K8, P6, K3, P2, K2, P2, K3, P6, K8, P8, K8, P6, K3, P2, K3.
Row 20: P4, K2, P2, K6, P8, K8, P8, K6, P2, K2, P2, K2, P2, K6, P8, K8, P8, K6, P2, K2, P4
Row 21: K5, P2, K1, P6, 2/2 LC, 2/2 RC, P8, 2/2 LC, 2/2 RC, P6, K1, P2, K6, P2, K1, P6, 2/2 LC, 2/2 RC, P8, 2/2 LC, 2/2 RC, P6, K1, P2, K5.
Row 22: P6, (K8, P8) five times, K8, P6.
Row 23: K7, P7, K8, P8, K8, P7, K10, P7, K8, P8, K8, P7, K7.
Row 24: P2, K1, P5, K6, P8, K8, P8, K6, P5, K2, P5, K6, P8, K8, P8, K6, P5, K1, P2.
Row 25: K2, P2, K4, P6, 2/2 LC, 2/2 RC, P8, 2/2 LC, 2/2 RC, P6, K4, P4, K4, P6, 2/2 LC, 2/2 RC, P8, 2/2 LC, 2/2 RC, P6, K4, P2, K2.
Row 26: P3, K2, P3, K6, P8, K8, P8, K6, P3, K2, P2, K2, P3, K6, P8, K8, P8, K6, P3, K2, P3.
Row 27: K4, P2, K2, P5, 2/1 RPC, P4, 2/1 LPC, P6, 2/1 RPC, P4, 2/1 LPC, P5, K2, P2, K4, P2, K2, P5, 2/1 RPC, P4, 2/1 LPC, P6, 2/1 RPC, P4, 2/1 LPC, P5, K2, P2, K4.
Row 28: P5, K2, P1, K5, (P2, K6) three times, P2, K5, P1, K2, P6, K2, P1, K5, (P2, K6) three times, P2, K5, P1, K2, P5.
Row 29: K6, P6, 2/1 RPC, P6, 2/1 LPC, P4, 2/1 RPC, P6, 2/1 LPC, P6, K8, P6, 2/1 RPC, P6, 2/1 LPC, P4, 2/1 RPC, P6, 2/1 LPC, P6, K6.
Row 30: P7, K5, P2, K8, P2, K4, P2, K8, P2, K5, P10, K5, P2, K8, P2, K4, P2, K8, P2, K5, P7.
After working Rows 1-30, rep Rows 3-30 for pattern.

Chart 1—Size 48" (flat over 108 sts)
Row 1 (RS): P2, (K8, P6, K2, P8, K2, P4, K2, P8, K2, P6) two times, K8, P2.
Row 2 (WS): K1, (P10, K5, P2, K8, P2, K4, P2, K8, P2, K5) two times, P10, K1.
Row 3: (K5, P2, K5, P2, 2/2 RC, P8, 2/2 LC, P2, 2/2 RC, P8, 2/2 LC, P2) two times, K5, P2, K5.
Row 4: (P4, K4, P4, K2, P4, K8, P8, K8, P4, K2) two times, P4, K4, P4.
Row 5: (K3, P2, K2, P2, K3, P2, K4, P8, K8, P8, K4, P2) two times, K3, P2, K2, P2, K3.
Row 6: (P2, K2, P4, K2, P2, K2, P4, K8, P8, K8, P4, K2) two times, P2, K2, P4, K2, P2.
Row 7: (K1, P2, K6, P2, K1, P2, 2/2 RC, P8, 2/2 LC, 2/2 RC, P8, 2/2 LC, P2) two times, K1, P2, K6, P2, K1.
Row 8: K2, (P8, K4, P4, K8, P8, K8, P4, K4) two times, P8, K2.
Row 9: P1, (K10, P3, K4, P8, K8, P8, K4, P3) two times, K10, P1.
Row 10: P5, K2, (P5, K2, P4, K8, P8, K8, P4, K2, P5, K2) two times, P5.
Row 11: (K4, P4, K4, P2, 2/2 RC, P8, 2/2 LC, 2/2 RC, P8, 2/2 LC, P2) two times, K4, P4, K4.
Row 12: (P3, K2, P2, K2, P3, K2, P4, K8, P8, K8, P4, K2) two times, P3, K2, P2, K2, P3.
Row 13: (K2, P2, K4, P2, K2, P4, 2/1 LPC, P6, 2/1 RPC, P4, 2/1 LPC, P6, 2/1 RPC, P4) two times, K2, P2, K4, P2, K2.
Row 14: (P1, K2, P6, K2, P1, K5, P2, K6, P2, K6, P2, K6, P2, K5) two times, P1, K2, P6, K2, P1.
Row 15: P2, (K8, P7, 2/1 LPC, P4, 2/1 RPC, P6, 2/1 LPC, P4, 2/1 RPC, P7) two times, K8, P2.
Row 16: K1, (P10, K7, P2, K4, P2, K8, P2, K4, P2, K7) two times, P10, K1.
Row 17: (K5, P2, K5, P6, 2/2 LC, 2/2 RC, P8, 2/2 LC, 2/2 RC, P6) two times, K5, P2, K5.
Row 18: (P4, K4, P4, K6, P8, K8, P8, K6) two times, P4, K4, P4.
Row 19: (K3, P2, K2, P2, K3, P6, K8, P8, K8, P6) two times, K3, P2, K2, P2, K3.

Row 20: (P2, K2, P4, K2, P2, K6, P8, K8, P8, K6) two times, P2, K2, P4, K2, P2.
Row 21: (K1, P2, K6, P2, K1, P6, 2/2 LC, 2/2 RC, P8, 2/2 LC, 2/2 RC, P6) two times, K1, P2, K6, P2, K1.
Row 22: K2, (P8, K8) six times, P8, K2.
Row 23: P1, (K10, P7, K8, P8, K8, P7) two times, K10, P1.
Row 24: (P5, K2, P5, K6, P8, K8, P8, K6) two times, P5, K2, P5.
Row 25: (K4, P4, K4, P6, 2/2 LC, 2/2 RC, P8, 2/2 LC, 2/2 RC, P6) two times, K4, P4, K4.
Row 26: (P3, K2, P2, K2, P3, K6, P8, K8, P8, K6) two times, P3, K2, P2, K2, P3.
Row 27: (K2, P2, K4, P2, K2, P5, 2/1 RPC, P4, 2/1 LPC, P6, 2/1 RPC, P4, 2/1 LPC, P5) two times, K2, P2, K4, P2, K2.
Row 28: (P1, K2, P6, K2, P1, K5, P2, K6, P2, K6, P2, K6, P2, K5) two times, P1, K2, P6, K2, P1.
Row 29: P2, (K8, P6, 2/1 RPC, P6, 2/1 LPC, P4, 2/1 RPC, P6, 2/1 LPC, P6) two times, K8, P2.
Row 30: K1, (P10, K5, P2, K8, P2, K4, P2, K8, P2, K5) two times, P10, K1.
After working Rows 1-30, rep Rows 3-30 for pattern.

Chart 1—Size 52" (flat over 116 sts)
Row 1 (RS): K4, P2, (K8, P6, K2, P8, K2, P4, K2, P8, K2, P6) two times, K8, P2, K4.
Row 2 (WS): P4, K1, (P10, K5, P2, K8, P2, K4, P2, K8, P2, K5) two times, P10, K1, P4.
Row 3: K9, (P2, K5, P2, 2/2 RC, P8, 2/2 LC, P2, 2/2 RC, P8, 2/2 LC, P2, K5) two times, P2, K9.
Row 4: P8, (K4, P4, K2, P4, K8, P8, K8, P4, K2, P4) two times, K4, P8.
Row 5: K7, P2, (K2, P2, K3, P2, K4, P8, K8, P8, K4, P2, K3, P2) two times, K2, P2, K7.
Row 6: P6, K2, (P4, K2, P2, K2, P4, K8, P8, K8, P4, K2, P2, K2) two times, P4, K2, P6.
Row 7: K5, P2, (K6, P2, K1, P2, 2/2 RC, P8, 2/2 LC, P8, 2/2 RC, P8, 2/2 LC, P2, K1, P2) two times, K6, P2, K5.
Row 8: P4, K2, (P8, K4, P4, K8, P8, K8, P4, K4) two times, P8, K2, P4.
Row 9: K4, P1, (K10, P3, K4, P8, K8, P8, K4, P3) two times, K10, P1, K4.
Row 10: P9, K2, (P5, K2, P4, K8, P8, K8, P4, K2, P5, K2) two times, P9.
Row 11: K8, (P4, K4, P2, 2/2 RC, P8, 2/2 LC, P8, 2/2 RC, P8, 2/2 LC, P2, K4) two times, P4, K8.
Row 12: P7, (K2, P2, K2, P3, K2, P4, K8, P8, K8, P4, K2, P3) two times, K2, P2, K2, P7.
Row 13: K6, (P2, K4, P2, K2, P4, 2/1 LPC, P6, 2/1 RPC, P4, 2/1 LPC, P6, 2/1 RPC, P4, K2) two times, P2, K4, P2, K6.
Row 14: P5, *K2, P6, K2, P1, K5, P2, (K6, P2) three times, K5, P1; rep from * one time, K2, P6, K2, P5.
Row 15: K4, P2, (K8, P7, 2/1 LPC, P4, 2/1 RPC, P6, 2/1 LPC, P4, 2/1 RPC, P7) two times, K8, P2, K4.
Row 16: P4, K1, (P10, K7, P2, K4, P2, K8, P2, K4, P2, K7) two times, P10, K1, P4.
Row 17: K9, P2, (K5, P6, 2/2 LC, 2/2 RC, P8, 2/2 LC, 2/2 RC, P6, K5, P2) two times, K9.
Row 18: P8, (K4, P4, K6, P8, K8, P8, K6, P4) two times, K4, P8.
Row 19: K7, (P2, K2, P2, K3, P6, K8, P8, K8, P6, K3) two times, P2, K2, P2, K7.
Row 20: P6, (K2, P4, K2, P2, K6, P8, K8, P8, K6, P2) two times, K2, P4, K2, P6.
Row 21: K5, (P2, K6, P2, K1, P6, 2/2 LC, 2/2 RC, P8, 2/2 LC, 2/2 RC, P6, K1) two times, P2, K6, P2, K5.
Row 22: P4, K2, (P8, K8) six times, P8, K2, P4.
Row 23: K4, P1, (K10, P7, K8, P8, K8, P7) two times, K10, P1, K4.
Row 24: P9, (K2, P5, K6, P8, K8, P8, K6, P5) two times, K2, P9.
Row 25: K8, (P4, K4, P6, 2/2 LC, 2/2 RC, P8, 2/2 LC, 2/2 RC, P6, K4) two times, P4, K8.
Row 26: P7, (K2, P2, K2, P3, K6, P8, K8, P8, K6, P3) two times, K2, P2, K2, P7.
Row 27: K6, (P2, K4, P2, K2, P5, 2/1 RPC, P4, 2/1 LPC, P6, 2/1 RPC, P4, 2/1 LPC, P5, K2) two times, P2, K4, P2, K6.
Row 28: P5, (K2, P6, K2, P1, K5, P2, K6, P2, K6, P2, K6, P2, K5, P1) two times, K2, P6, K2, P5.
Row 29: K4, P2, (K8, P6, 2/1 RPC, P6, 2/1 LPC, P4, 2/1 RPC, P6, 2/1 LPC, P6) two times, K8, P2, K4.
Row 30: P4, K1, (P10, K5, P2, K8, P2, K4, P2, K8, P2, K5) two times, P10, K1, P4.
After working Rows 1-30, rep Rows 3-30 for pattern.

Chart 2 (in the round over 74 (78, 82, 86, 90, 90) sts)
Rnd 1 (RS): K3 (5, 7, 9, 11, 11), P2, (P2, K2, P8, K2, P2) four times, P2, K3 (5, 7, 9, 11, 11).
Rnd 2: K3 (5, 7, 9, 11, 11), P2, (P2, K2, P8, K2, P2) four times, P2, K3 (5, 7, 9, 11, 11).
Rnd 3: K3 (5, 7, 9, 11, 11), P2, (2/2 RC, P8, 2/2 LC) four times, P2, K3 (5, 7, 9, 11, 11).
Rnd 4: K3 (5, 7, 9, 11, 11), P2, (K4, P8, K4) four times, P2, K3 (5, 7, 9, 11, 11).
Rnd 5: K3 (5, 7, 9, 11, 11), P2, (K4, P8, K4) four times, P2, K3 (5, 7, 9, 11, 11).
Rnd 6: K3 (5, 7, 9, 11, 11), P2, (K4, P8, K4) four times, P2, K3 (5, 7, 9, 11, 11).
Rnd 7: K3 (5, 7, 9, 11, 11), P2, (2/2 RC, P8, 2/2 LC) four times, P2, K3 (5, 7, 9, 11, 11).
Rnd 8: K3 (5, 7, 9, 11, 11), P2, (K4, P8, K4) four times, P2, K3 (5, 7, 9, 11, 11).
Rnd 9: K3 (5, 7, 9, 11, 11), P2, (K4, P8, K4) four times, P2, K3 (5, 7, 9, 11, 11).
Rnd 10: K3 (5, 7, 9, 11, 11), P2, (K4, P8, K4) four times, P2, K3 (5, 7, 9, 11, 11).
Rnd 11: K3 (5, 7, 9, 11, 11), P2, (2/2 RC, P8, 2/2 LC) four times, P2, K3 (5, 7, 9, 11, 11).
Rnd 12: K3 (5, 7, 9, 11, 11), P2, (K4, P8, K4) four times, P2, K3 (5, 7, 9, 11, 11).
Rnd 13: K3 (5, 7, 9, 11, 11), P2, (P2, 2/1 LPC, P6, 2/1 RPC, P2) four times, P2, K3 (5, 7, 9, 11, 11).
Rnd 14: K3 (5, 7, 9, 11, 11), P2, (P3, K2, P6, K2, P3) four times, P2, K3 (5, 7, 9, 11, 11).
Rnd 15: K3 (5, 7, 9, 11, 11), P2, (P3, 2/1 LPC, P4, 2/1 RPC, P3) four times, P2, K3 (5, 7, 9, 11, 11).
Rnd 16: K3 (5, 7, 9, 11, 11), P2, (P4, K2, P4, K2, P4) four times, P2, K3 (5, 7, 9, 11, 11).

Pleinmont 75

Rnd 17: K3 (5, 7, 9, 11, 11), P2, (P4, 2/2 LC, 2/2 RC, P4) four times, P2, K3 (5, 7, 9, 11, 11).
Rnd 18: K3 (5, 7, 9, 11, 11), P2, (P4, K8, P4) four times, P2, K3 (5, 7, 9, 11, 11).
Rnd 19: K3 (5, 7, 9, 11, 11), P2, (P4, K8, P4) four times, P2, K3 (5, 7, 9, 11, 11).
Rnd 20: K3 (5, 7, 9, 11, 11), P2, (P4, K8, P4) four times, P2, K3 (5, 7, 9, 11, 11).
Rnd 21: K3 (5, 7, 9, 11, 11), P2, (P4, 2/2 LC, 2/2 RC, P4) four times, P2, K3 (5, 7, 9, 11, 11).

DIRECTIONS

Body
With smaller size needles, CO 128 (144, 160, 176, 192, 208) sts. PM and join to work in the rnd, being careful not to twist sts. Work 2x2 Rib for 2.25 (2.25, 2.5, 2.5, 2.75, 2.75)".
Switch to larger size needles. Work St st until Body measures 15.5 (16, 16.5, 17, 17.5, 18)" from CO edge.

Armhole Divide
P across 64 (72, 80, 88, 96, 104) Back sts. Place remaining sts on holder for Front. Turn to work flat.

Back
Row 1 (WS): K across. 64 (72, 80, 88, 96, 104) sts.
Row 2 (RS): K across, increasing 10 (10, 12, 12, 12, 12) sts evenly across. 74 (82, 92, 100, 108, 116) sts.
Row 3: P across.
Work Rows 1-30 of Chart 1 for chosen size.
Rep Chart 1 Rows 3-30 until armhole measures 7.5 (8, 8.5, 9, 9.5, 9.5)", ending with a WS row.

Shape Right Back Neck
Row 1 (RS): Work in pattern for 21 (25, 28, 32, 35, 38) sts, then place remaining sts on holder. Turn to cont work on these sts.
Row 2 (WS): P2tog, work in pattern to end. 20 (24, 27, 31, 34, 37) sts.
Row 3: BO 10 (12, 13, 15, 17, 18) sts in pattern, work in pattern to last 2 sts, K2tog. 29 (35, 39, 50, 54) sts.
Row 4: BO remaining 9 (11, 13, 15, 16, 18) sts in pattern.

Shape Left Back Neck
Setup Row (WS): Place 21 (25, 28, 32, 35, 38) left back sts onto needles, leaving 32 (32, 36, 36, 38, 40) center sts on holder; with WS facing, attach yarn at shoulder edge and work 21 (25, 28, 32, 35, 38) sts in WS pattern. Turn to work on these sts.
Row 1 (RS): SSK, work in pattern to end.
Row 2 (WS): BO 10 (12, 13, 15, 17, 18) sts in pattern, work in pattern to last 2 sts, P2tog.
Row 3: BO remaining 9 (11, 13, 15, 16, 18) sts in pattern.

Front
Attach yarn at left front armhole and P64 (72, 80, 88, 96, 104) sts. Turn to work flat.
Row 1 (WS): K across.
Row 2 (RS): K across, increasing 10 (10, 12, 12, 12, 12) sts evenly. 74 (82, 92, 100, 108, 116) sts.
Row 3: P across.
Work rows 1-30 of Chart 1 for chosen size.
Rep Chart 1 Rows 3-30 until armhole measures 5.5 (6, 6.5, 7, 7.5, 7.5)", ending with a WS row.

Shape Left Front Neck
Row 1 (RS): Work in pattern for 30 (34, 37, 41, 44, 47) sts, then place remaining sts on holder. Turn to cont work on these sts.
Row 2 (WS): BO 4 sts, work in pattern to end. 26 (30, 33, 37, 40, 43) sts.
Dec 1 st at neck edge of next five rows, then 1 st on next two RS rows. 19 (23, 26, 30, 33, 36) sts.
Work three rows in pattern.
Next Row (RS): BO 10 (12, 13, 15, 17, 18) sts in pattern, work in pattern to end of row.
Next Row: BO remaining 9 (11, 13, 15, 16, 18) sts in pattern.

Shape Right Front Neck
Setup Row (RS): Leaving 14 (14, 18, 18, 20, 22) center sts on holder, attach yarn at right neck edge and BO 4 sts, then work 26 (30, 33, 37, 40, 43) sts in pattern. Turn to work on these sts.
Dec 1 st at neck edge of next five rows, then on next two RS rows. 19 (23, 26, 30, 33, 36) sts.
Work four more rows in pattern.
Next Row (WS): BO 10 (12, 13, 15, 17, 18) sts in pattern, work in pattern to end of row.
Next Row: BO remaining 9 (11, 13, 15, 16, 18) sts in pattern.

Sleeves (make two the same)
Using smaller size DPNs, loosely CO 36 (36, 36, 40, 40, 40) sts. PM and join to work in the rnd, being careful not to twist sts. Work 2x2 Rib for 2.25 (2.25, 2.5, 2.5, 2.75, 2.75)".
Switch to larger size DPNs. Work St st for one rnd, increasing 4 sts evenly around. 40 (40, 40, 44, 44, 44) sts.
Cont in St st, increasing 1 st at beginning and end of every 4 (4, 3, 3, 3, 3) rnds 11 (13, 15, 15, 17, 17) times. 62 (66, 70, 74, 78, 78) sts.
Switch to larger size 16" circular needles when sleeve circumference is large enough to fit.
Cont in St st until sleeve measures 13 (13.5, 13.5, 14, 14, 14.5)" from CO edge.
Work Rev St st for two rnds.
Work St st for one rnd, increasing 12 sts evenly around. 74 (78, 82, 86, 90, 90) sts.
Work St st for one more rnd.
Beginning each rnd of Chart 2 as marked for chosen size, work pattern rep four times, then work to end of rnd as marked for chosen size. Work Rnds 1-21 once for all sizes. BO loosely in pattern. Break yarn, leaving long tail for finishing.

Finishing
Sew back to front at shoulder seams.
Pin sleeves into armhole of sweater, stretching sleeve to fit as necessary. Sew sleeves into sweater body.

Neck Band

Beginning at right shoulder seam with smaller size 16" needles, PU and K 3 sts along right back, place 32 (32, 36, 36, 38, 40) center back sts from holder onto needle and K across, PU and K 3 sts along left back, PU and K 12 sts along left front, place 14 (14, 18, 18, 20, 22) center front sts from holder onto needle and K across, PU and K 12 sts along right front. 76 (76, 84, 84, 88, 92) sts. PM and join to work in the rnd. Work 2x2 Rib for 2".
BO loosely in pattern.

Weave in ends, wash, and block to diagram.

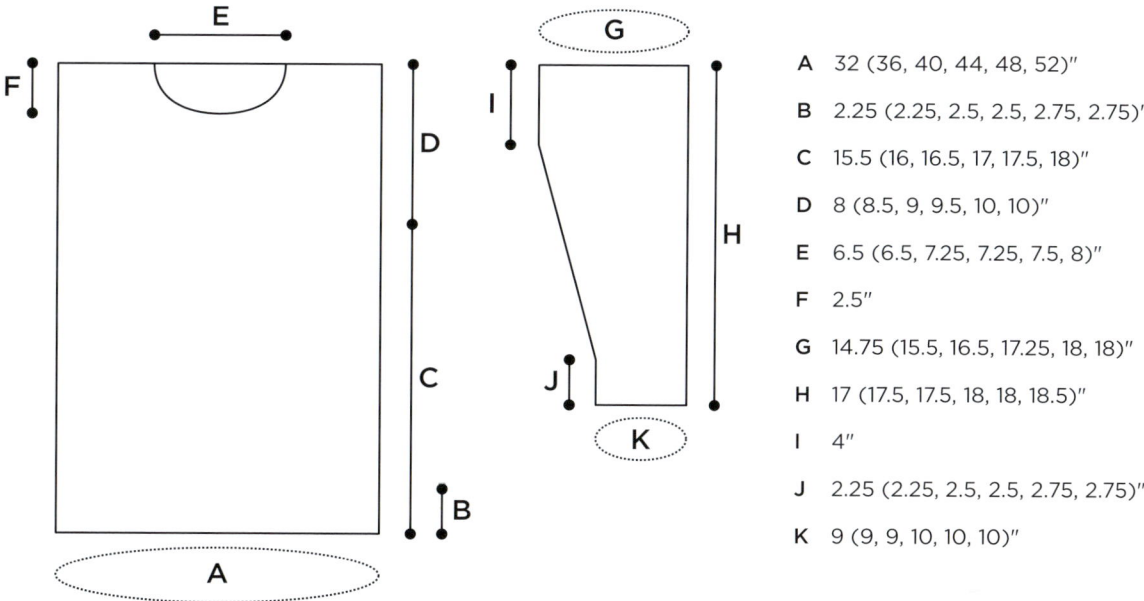

A 32 (36, 40, 44, 48, 52)"
B 2.25 (2.25, 2.5, 2.5, 2.75, 2.75)" (hem)
C 15.5 (16, 16.5, 17, 17.5, 18)"
D 8 (8.5, 9, 9.5, 10, 10)"
E 6.5 (6.5, 7.25, 7.25, 7.5, 8)"
F 2.5"
G 14.75 (15.5, 16.5, 17.25, 18, 18)"
H 17 (17.5, 17.5, 18, 18, 18.5)"
I 4"
J 2.25 (2.25, 2.5, 2.5, 2.75, 2.75)"
K 9 (9, 9, 10, 10, 10)"

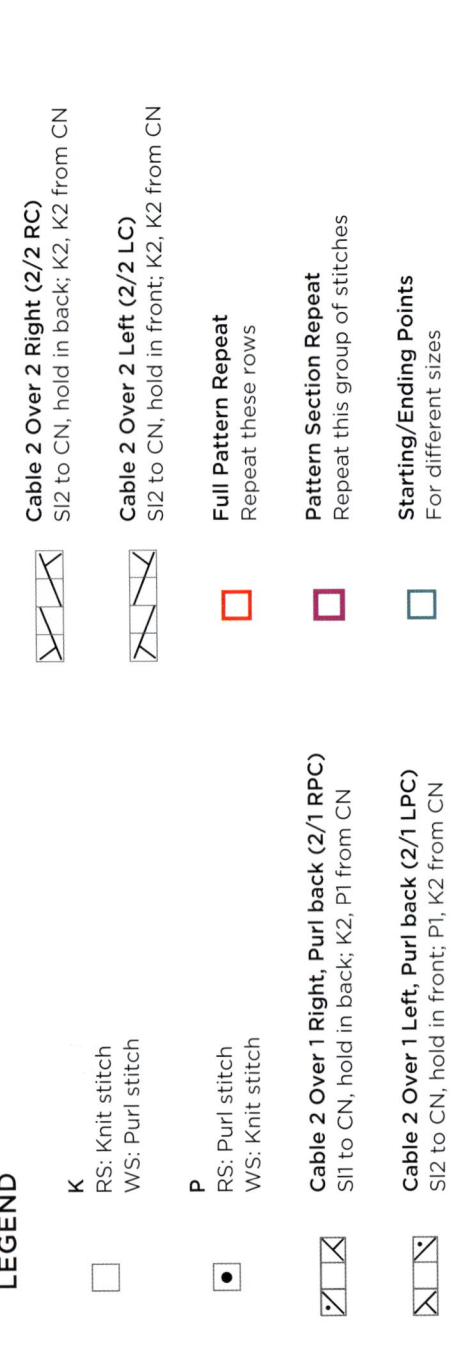

Pleinmont Chart 1—Size 32" & 36"

LEGEND

K
RS: Knit stitch
WS: Purl stitch

P
RS: Purl stitch
WS: Knit stitch

Cable 2 Over 1 Right, Purl back (2/1 RPC)
Sl1 to CN, hold in back; K2, P1 from CN

Cable 2 Over 1 Left, Purl back (2/1 LPC)
Sl2 to CN, hold in front; P1, K2 from CN

Cable 2 Over 2 Right (2/2 RC)
Sl2 to CN, hold in back; K2, K2 from CN

Cable 2 Over 2 Left (2/2 LC)
Sl2 to CN, hold in front; K2, K2 from CN

Full Pattern Repeat
Repeat these rows

Pattern Section Repeat
Repeat this group of stitches

Starting/Ending Points
For different sizes

Pleinmont Chart 1—Size 40" & 44"

Pleinmont Chart 1—Size 48" & 52"

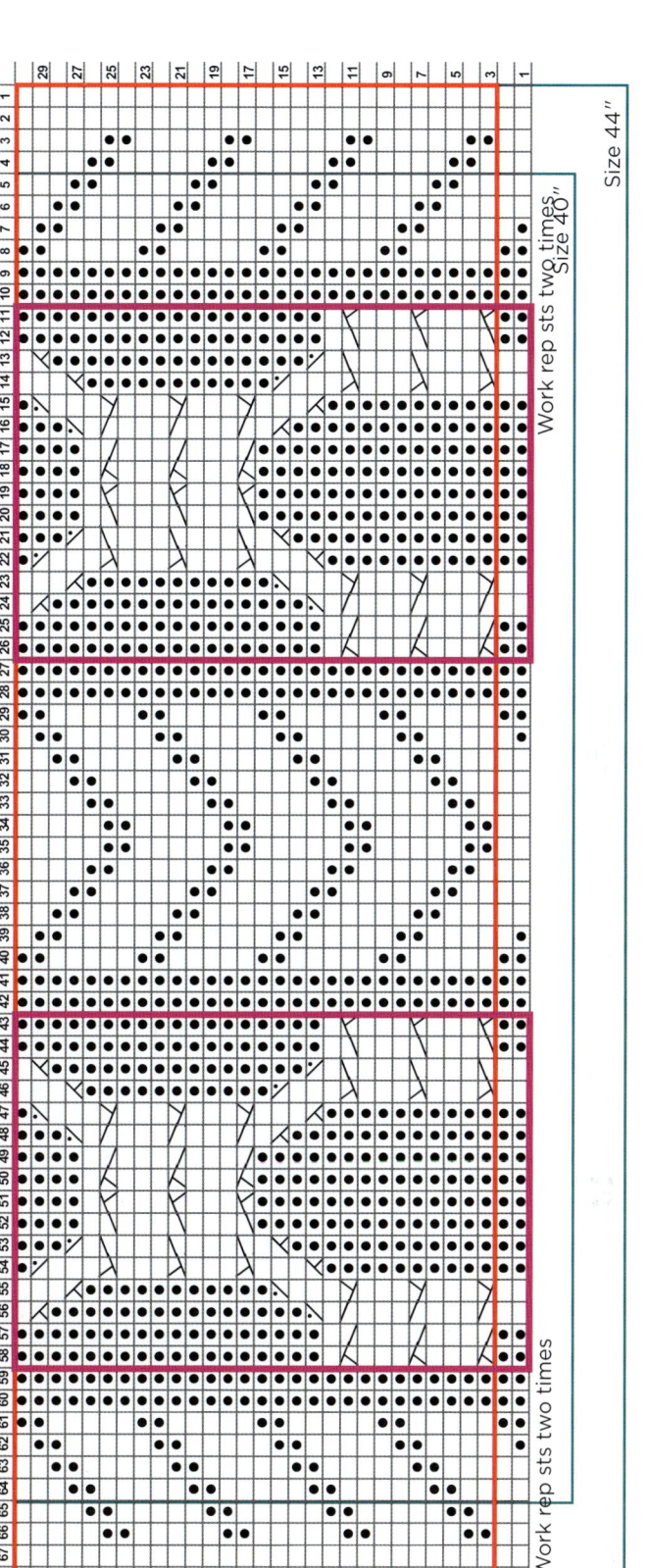

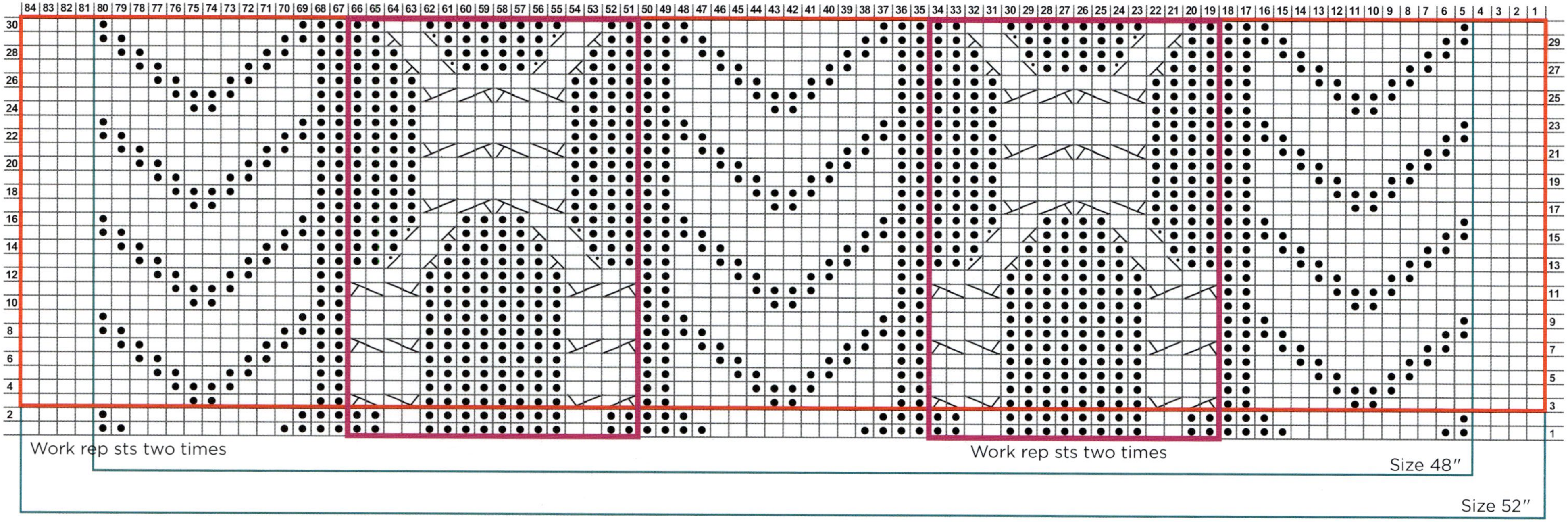

Pleinmont 79

Pleinmont Chart 2

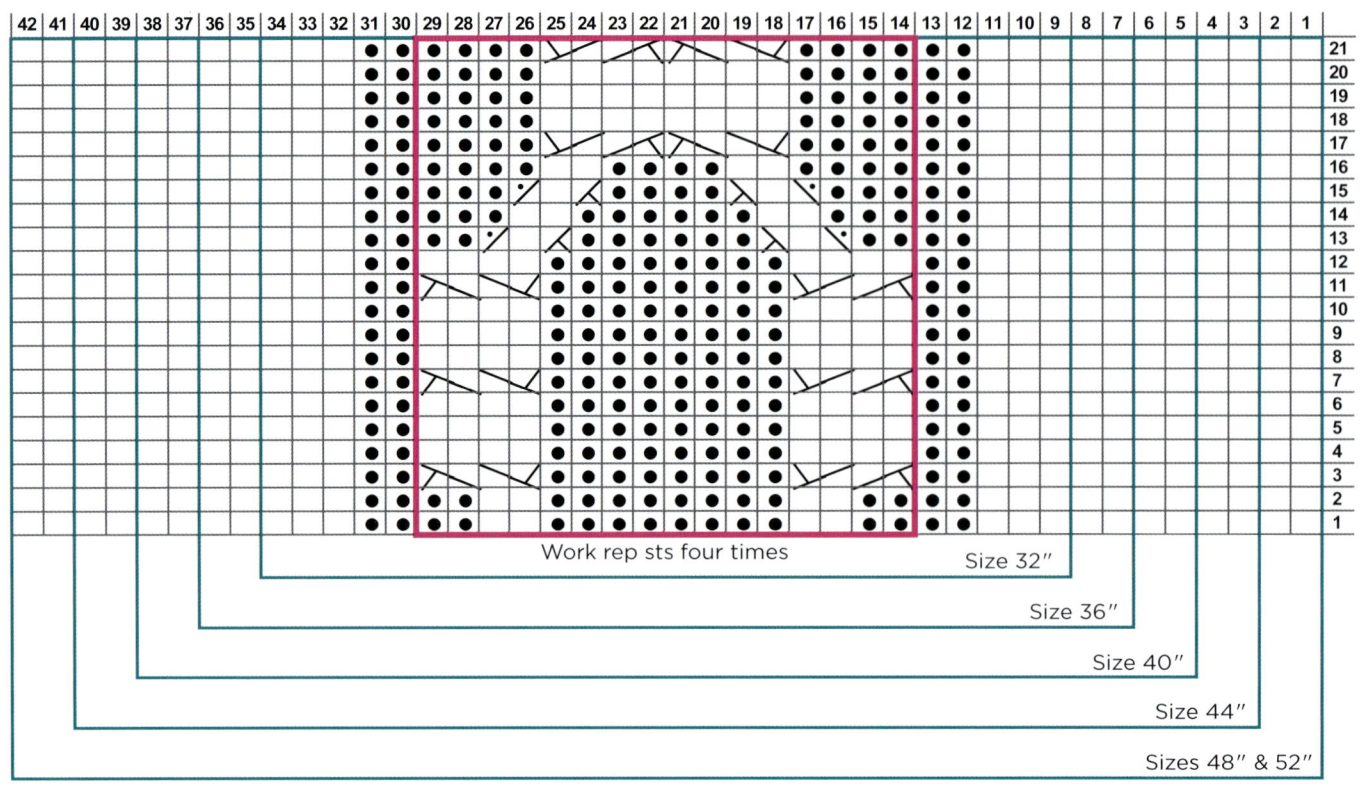

Neckband

Using circular needles or DPNs, with RS of work facing, beginning at back right shoulder, PU and K 45 (49, 53, 59, 63, 69, 71, 75, 77) sts along back neck, PU and K 17 (17, 17, 20, 20, 20, 24, 24, 24) sts along left side of front neck, PU and K 33 (37, 41, 45, 49, 53, 53, 57, 57) sts for front neck, PU and K 17 (17, 17, 20, 20, 20, 24, 24, 24) sts along right side of front neck. 112 (120, 128, 144, 152, 162, 172, 180, 182) sts.
Join to work in the rnd.
Work 1x1 Rib for 15 (15, 15, 19, 19, 19, 23, 23, 23) rnds.
BO all sts loosely.
Break yarn, leaving a long tail. Fold neckband to inside and use yarn tail to join to first row of the ribbed section on the inside.

Finishing

Using Mattress Stitch and referring to schematic, attach sleeves to body. Use Mattress Stitch to join side seams and underarms seams.
Weave in ends. Wash and block sweater, referring to schematic for measurements.

Right Side will be worked over these sts. Rep as for Left Side of neck from * to end of section (which rows are RS/WS will be opposite from Left Side).

Sleeves (work two the same)
Cuff
CO 50 (50, 54, 54, 58, 58, 58, 62, 62) sts.
Work Rows 1-27 of Chart A once.
Row 28 (WS): K5 (5, 1, 1, 3, 3, 3, 5, 5), *M1, K3 (3, 4, 4, 4, 4, 4, 4, 4); rep from * twelve more times, K6 (6, 1, 1, 3, 3, 3, 5, 5). 63 (63, 67, 67, 71, 71, 71, 75, 75) sts.

Read through this section before beginning because incs and patterning are worked at the same time. Incorporate inc sts into established chart pattern.
Inc Row (RS): K1, M1, work in pattern to last st, M1, K1. 2 sts inc.
Work Inc Row every fourth row 0 (0, 0, 6, 0, 8, 16, 17, 29) times, then every sixth row 0 (8, 9, 18, 23, 18, 13, 13, 6) times, then every eighth row 14 (9, 9, 0, 0, 0, 0, 0, 0) times. 91 (97, 103, 115, 117, 123, 129, 135, 145) sts.

AT THE SAME TIME, work Rows 1-10 of Chart B 4 (5, 5, 6, 6, 6, 6, 7, 7) times, then work Rows 1-5 of Chart B 1 (0, 1, 0, 1, 1, 1, 0, 0) time(s). 45 (50, 55, 60, 65, 65, 65, 70, 70) rows have been worked. 73 (79, 85, 91, 91, 97, 103, 109, 109) sts.
Work Rows 1-6 of Chart C once.
Next Row (RS): Work last 7 (0, 3, 1, 7, 4, 4, 8, 5, 6) sts of Row 1 of Chart D, work all sts of Row 1 of Chart D 3 (4, 4, 4, 4, 4, 4, 5, 5) times, work Row 1 of Chart E1 once, work Row 1 of Chart F once, work Row 1 of Chart E2 once, work Row 1 of Chart G 3 (4, 4, 4, 4, 4, 4, 5, 5) times, then work first 7 (0, 3, 1, 7, 4, 4, 8, 5, 6) sts of Chart G.

Next Row (WS): Work first 7 (0, 3, 1, 7, 4, 4, 8, 5, 6) sts of Row 2 of Chart G, work all sts of Row 2 of Chart G 3 (4, 4, 4, 4, 4, 4, 5, 5) times, work Row 2 of Chart E2 once, work Row 2 of Chart F once, work Row 2 of Chart E1 once, work Row 2 of Chart D 3 (4, 4, 4, 4, 4, 4, 5, 5) times, then work last 7 (0, 3, 1, 7, 4, 4, 8, 5, 6) sts of Chart D.
Cont in pattern as established until sleeve measures 12.75 (13.75, 14.25, 15.25, 15.75, 16.25, 16.25, 16.75, 17.25)".
Work Chart C once.
BO all sts.

Shoulders
With RS of front facing, place left side 33 (37, 41, 44, 48, 51, 56, 60, 65) shoulder sts on needle. With WS of back facing, place left side 33 (37, 41, 44, 48, 51, 56, 60, 65) shoulder sts on second needle. With RSs of work facing inward, work 3-Needle Bind Off.
Rep for right side shoulder.

A 37 (41, 45, 49, 53, 57, 61, 65, 69)"

B 13.25 (14.25, 14.75, 15.75, 16.25, 16.75, 16.75, 17.25, 17.75)"

C 15 (16, 17, 19, 19.5, 20.5, 21.5, 22.5, 24)"

D 8.25 (8.5, 8.75, 9, 9.25, 9.5, 9.75, 10, 10.5)"

E 2 (2, 2, 2.5, 2.5, 2.5, 3, 3, 3)"

F 10 (10.5, 11, 11.5, 12, 13, 13.5, 14, 14.5)"

G 16.5 (18, 19.5, 19.5, 21.25, 21.75, 22.25, 22.25, 22)"

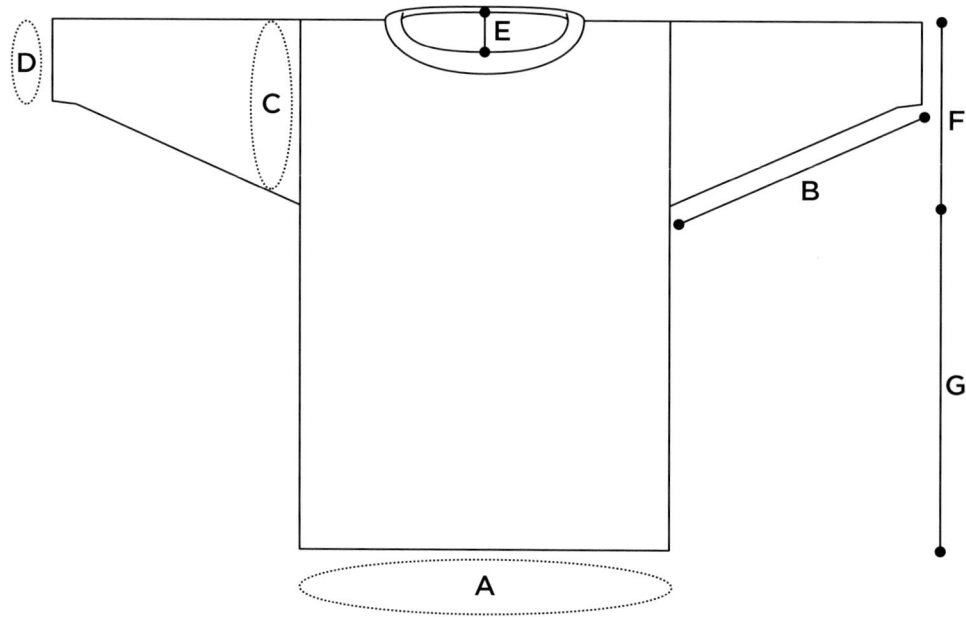

Sandy Road

Notes:

This sweater is a tribute to the traditional gansey sweaters worn by British fisherman in the 19th and 20th centuries. The sweater motifs are said to represent a particular village or family, making identification of those lost at sea an easier, albeit tragic, task.

Sandy Road is an oversized, long sleeve, hip length, unisex gansey-style sweater designed to be worn with 6-8" of positive ease. There are six different motifs worked across the body and sleeves. All pieces are worked flat and sewn together at the end, and the neck stitches are bound off rather than put on hold. At the neck edges, stitches are bound off rather than decreased.

Picking up the stitches around the neck, the 3-Needle Bind Off at the shoulders, and the sewn seams provide this garment with structure, which may not be present if knitted in the round with grafted shoulders. The front and back are worked from the bottom up and are identical, apart from the neck shaping; the sleeves are worked flat from the cuffs up.

It may be easier to use circular needles than straight needles to accommodate the number of stitches, particularly for the body pieces. It may be useful to use stitch markers for the yoke and the top of the sleeves where several different patterns are worked in the same row.

Charts are worked flat; read RS rows (odd numbers) from right to left, and WS rows (even numbers) from left to right.

When instructions state to work a given chart, work across the row, ending (RS) or beginning (WS) with a partial chart row as needed.

DIRECTIONS

Body

Back

*Using gauge size needles of your choice, CO 110 (122, 134, 146, 158, 170, 182, 194, 206) sts.
Work Rows 1-27 of Chart A once.
Row 28 (WS): K55 (61, 67, 73, 79, 85, 91, 97, 103), M1, K to end. 111 (123, 135, 147, 159, 171, 183, 195, 207) sts.

Next Row (RS): Work Chart B Row 1 beginning at St 2 (6, 10, 4, 8, 2, 6, 10, 4), then rep Chart B to end, working partial chart as needed at end.
Work in pattern, rep Rows 1-10 of Chart B until piece measures 13.5 (15, 16.5, 17, 18, 18, 18, 18, 19)" from start, ending with Row 10.
Work Rows 1-6 of Chart B 1 (0, 1, 0, 1, 1, 0, 0, 0) more time(s).
Work Chart C Rows 1-6 once.

Next Row (RS): Work last 4 (2, 0, 3, 1, 7, 2, 0, 6) sts of Row 1 of Chart D, then work all sts of Row 1 of Chart D 5 (6, 7, 7, 8, 8, 9, 10, 10) times, work Row 1 of Chart E1 once, work Row 1 of Chart F once, work Row 1 of Chart E2 once, work Row 1 of Chart G 5 (6, 7, 7, 8, 8, 9, 10 10) times, then work first 4 (2, 0, 3, 1, 7, 2, 0, 6) sts of Chart G Row 1. Be sure to work E Charts for your size.
Next Row (WS): Work first 4 (2, 0, 3, 1, 7, 2, 0, 6) sts of Row 2 of Chart G, then work all sts of Row 2 Chart G 5 (6, 7, 7, 8, 8, 9, 10, 10) times, work Row 2 of Chart E2 once, work Row 2 of Chart F once, work Row 2 of Chart E1 once, work Row 2 of Chart D 5 (6, 7, 7, 8, 8, 9, 10, 10) times, then work last 4 (2, 0, 3, 1, 7, 2, 0, 6) sts of Row 2 of Chart D.*
Cont in pattern as established, working charts until piece measures 26.5 (28.5, 30.5, 31, 33.25, 34.75, 35.75, 36.25, 36.5)" from CO edge, ending with a WS row.
Next Row (RS): Work 33 (37, 41, 44, 48, 51, 56, 60, 65) sts in pattern then place them on st holder or spare yarn, BO next 45 (49, 53, 59, 63, 69, 71, 75, 77) sts, work 33 (37, 41, 44, 48, 51, 56, 60, 65) remaining sts then place them on st holder or spare yarn.
Put Back aside and work Front.

Front

Rep as for Back from * to *.
Cont in pattern as established, working charts until piece measures 24.5 (26.5, 28.5, 28.5, 30.75, 32.25, 32.75, 33.25, 33.5)" from CO edge, ending with a WS row.

Left Side Neck Shaping

Cont working charts in pattern as established and at the same time, with RS facing, shape LH side of neck as follows:
Row 1 (RS): Work 39 (43, 47, 51, 55, 59, 65, 69, 75) sts in pattern, turn. (LH side will be worked over these 39 (43, 47, 51, 55, 59, 65, 69, 75) sts.)
*Next Row: BO 1 st, work in pattern to end. 1 st dec.
Next Row: Work in pattern to end.
Next Row: BO 1 st, work in pattern to end. 1 st dec.
Work the last two rows 1 (1, 1, 1, 2, 2, 2, 3) more time(s). 36 (40, 44, 48, 52, 55, 61, 65, 70) sts.
Next Row: Work in pattern to end.
Next Row: BO 1 st, work in pattern to end. 1 st dec.
Work two rows in pattern.
Work last four rows 2 (2, 2, 3, 3, 3, 4, 4, 4) more times. 33 (37, 41, 44, 48, 51, 56, 60, 65) sts.
Work even for 4 (4, 4, 4, 4, 2, 4, 4, 2) more rows.
Break yarn and place remaining 33 (37, 41, 44, 48, 51, 56, 60, 65) sts on holder.

Neck Bind Off

With RS facing, rejoin yarn and BO next 33 (37, 41, 45, 49, 53, 53, 57, 57) sts (center of neck), work charts in pattern to end.

Right Side Neck Shaping

Next Row (WS): Work remaining 39 (43, 47, 51, 55, 59, 65, 69, 75) sts in pattern as established.

SANDY ROAD

by Beverley Dott

FINISHED MEASUREMENTS
37 (41, 45, 49, 53, 57, 61, 65, 69)" finished chest circumference; meant to be worn with 6-8" positive ease

YARN
Knit Picks Swish™ (DK weight, 100% Fine Superwash Merino Wool; 123 yards/50g): Garnet Heather 24315, 13 (14, 17, 19, 22, 24, 26, 28, 29) skeins

NEEDLES
US 3 (3.25mm) straight or circular needles (24" or longer), or size to obtain gauge
US 3 (3.25mm) 16" circular needles or DPNs (for neckband), or size to obtain gauge
US 3 (3.25mm) extra needle for 3-Needle Bind Off

NOTIONS
Yarn Needle
Stitch Markers (extras can be useful)
Scrap Yarn or Stitch Holders

GAUGE
24 sts and 42 rows = 4" in Chart B Pattern, worked flat and blocked

For pattern support, contact faircityknits@outlook.com

LEGEND

K
RS: Knit stitch
WS: Purl stitch

P
RS: Purl stitch
WS: Knit stitch

Pattern Repeat

Sizes 37", 41" & 45"

Sizes 49", 53" & 57"

Sizes 61", 65" & 69"

Chart B

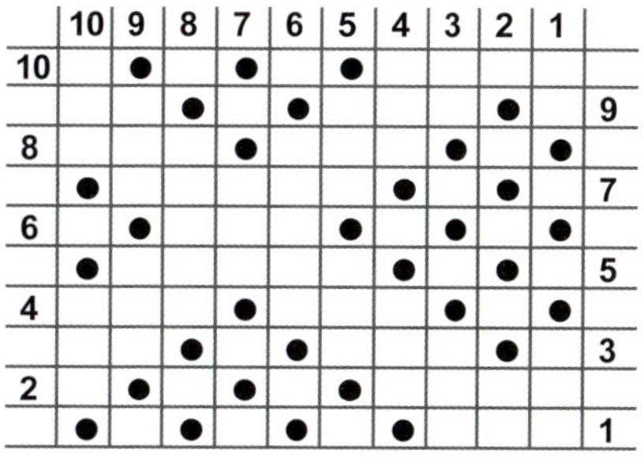

Chart C

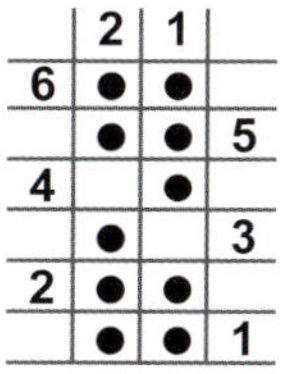

Chart D

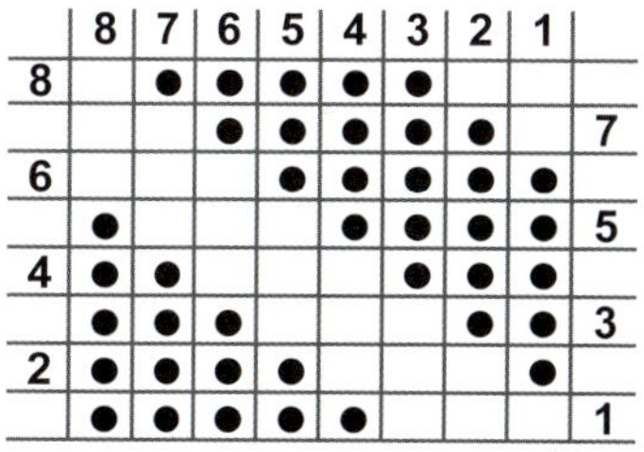

Chart A

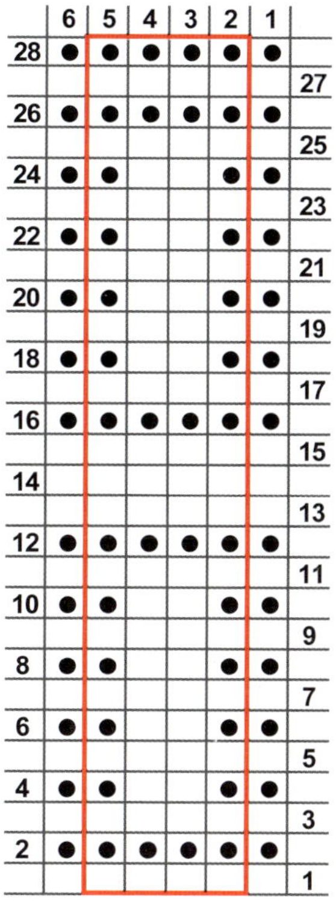

Chart E1

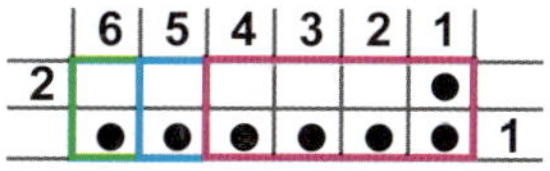

Chart E2

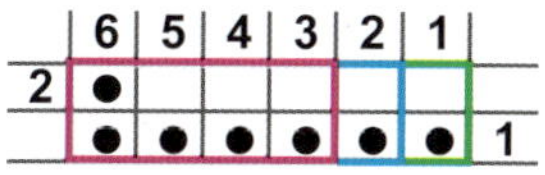

Chart F

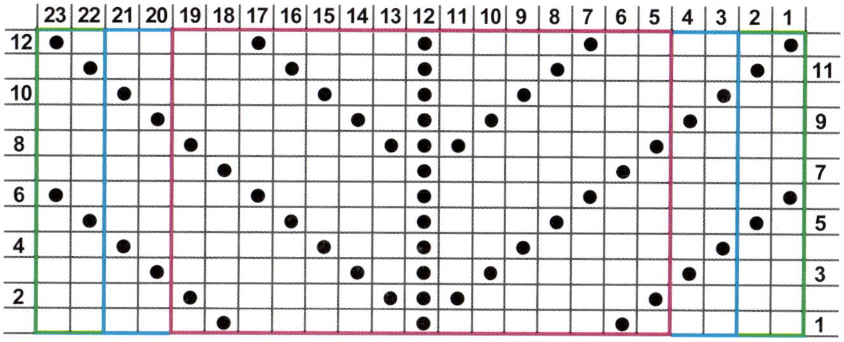

Chart G

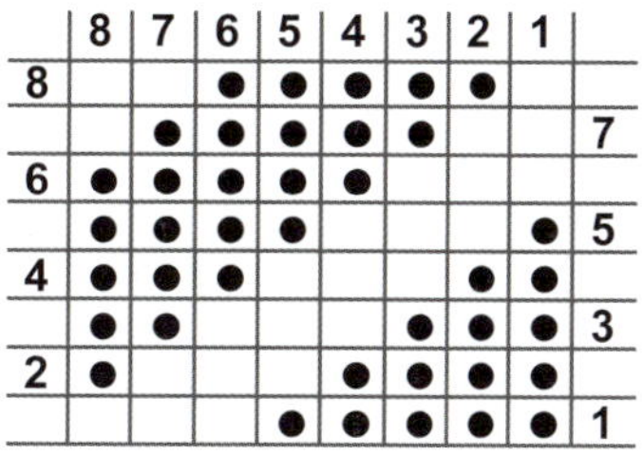

ST. MARTIN'S GUERNSEY

by Donna Estin

FINISHED MEASUREMENTS
32 (36, 40, 44, 48, 52, 56)" finished chest circumference; meant to be worn with 2-4" positive ease

YARN
Knit Picks Simply Wool™ (worsted weight, 100% Eco Wool; 218 yards/100g): Wanda 27468, 5 (6, 7, 7, 8, 9, 10) hanks

NEEDLES
US 8 (5mm) DPNs or two 24" circular needles for two circulars technique, or size to obtain gauge
US 8 (5mm) 32" circular needles, or size to obtain gauge
US 7 (4.5mm) 16" circular needles, or one size smaller than size used to obtain gauge

NOTIONS
Yarn Needle
Stitch Markers
Cable Needle
Scrap Yarn or Stitch Holders

GAUGE
19 sts and 28 rows = 4" in Stockinette Stitch on larger needles, blocked
15-st panel of Chart C = 3.5"
10-st panel of Charts B & D = 1.5"

For pattern support, contact donnaestindesigns@gmail.com

St. Martin's Guernsey

Notes:
Inspired by the parish of St. Martin in Guernsey, Channel Islands, this unisex pullover is designed with the traditional look of a guernsey but is knit in a style more familiar for today's knitters.

The deep waistband is worked in a textured rib and includes classic side vents for ease and mobility. Body and set-in sleeves are worked in the round from the bottoms up and divided at the armholes, then worked flat. It is designed to provide a standard fit for men and a looser fit for women.

Charts are worked both flat and in the round. When working charts in the round, read each chart row from right to left as a RS row. When working charts flat, read RS rows (odd numbers) from right to left, and WS rows (even numbers) from left to right.

Garter Ridge (in the round over any number of sts)
Rnd 1: P all.
Rnd 2: Rep Rnd 1.
Rnd 3: K all.
Rnd 4: Rep Rnd 3.
Rnd 5: P all.
Rnd 6: Rep Rnd 5.

Kitchener Rib Bind Off
Setup: Cut yarn, leaving a tail 3-4 times width of ribbing, and thread onto a tapestry needle. With first st a K st, insert tapestry needle P-wise into first st and draw yarn through. Insert needle from behind work, between first and second sts, and insert K-wise into front of second st (which is a P st) and pull yarn through.
Step 1: Insert needle K-wise into first K st and drop it from needle.
Step 2: Insert needle P-wise into next K st and pull yarn through.
Step 3: Insert needle P-wise into first P st and drop it from needle.
Step 4: Bring needle behind first st, insert it K-wise into next P st, and pull yarn through.
Rep Steps 1-4 until 2 sts remain. Insert needle K-wise into last K st and drop it from needle. Insert needle P-wise into last st and drop it from needle. Pull yarn snug.

German Short Rows (GSR) (on a RS row)
Turn work, WYIF slip next st P-wise and pull yarn up snugly. Wrap yarn behind RH needle and down through needles (making a "double stitch") to P next st.

German Short Rows (GSR) (on a WS row)
Turn work, WYIF slip next st P-wise and pull yarn up snugly. Pull yarn to back (making a "double stitch") to K next st.

DIRECTIONS

Body
Hem
With larger circular needles, CO 78 (86, 97, 105, 116, 124, 135) sts. Drop yarn; with second ball, CO 78 (86, 97, 105, 116, 124, 135) sts. Work both hems flat, at the same time, as follows:
Row 1 (RS): *K1, work Row 1 of Chevron—Left chart 0 (1, 0, 1, 0, 1, 0) times over 0 (4, 0, 4, 0, 4, 0) sts, work Row 1 of Chevron Rib chart 4 (4, 5, 5, 6, 6, 7) times over center 76 (76, 95, 95, 114, 114, 133) sts, work Row 1 of Chevron—Right chart 0 (1, 0, 1, 0, 1, 0) times over 0 (4, 0, 4, 0, 4, 0) sts, K1; rep from * for second hem with other ball of yarn.
Row 2 (WS): *K1, work Row 2 of Chevron—Right 0 (1, 0, 1, 0, 1, 0) times, work Row 2 of Chevron Rib 4 (4, 5, 5, 6, 6, 7) times, work Row 2 of Chevron—Left 0 (1, 0, 1, 0, 1, 0) times, K1; rep from * for second hem with other ball of yarn. Maintaining first and last st of every row in Garter st, cont to work all rows; rep until hem measures approx 4", ending with a chart Row 4.

Sizes 32", 40", 48" & 56" Only
*K24 (-, 31, -, 38, -, 43), K2tog, K26 (-, 31, -, 36, -, 45), K2tog, K to end of first hem, rep from * with same yarn, across second hem. Join in the rnd, careful not to twist, and PM for BOR. 152(-, 190, -, 228, -, 266) sts.

Sizes 26", 44" & 52" Only
K to end of first hem, K with same yarn to end of second hem. Join in the rnd, careful not to twist, and PM for BOR. - (172, -, 210, -, 248, -) sts.

Main Body
Break non-working yarn.
Work in St st until piece measures 16 (16, 17, 17, 17, 18, 18)" from CO edge.
Work in Garter Ridge for 5 (6, 5, 5, 6, 6, 5) rnds.

Size 32" Only
Inc Rnd: (K38, M1) to end. 156 sts.

Sizes 40", 44" & 56" Only
Inc Rnd: *K- (-, 95, 105, -, -, 133), M1; rep from * to end. - (-, 192, 212, -, -, 268) sts.

All Sizes Resume
Next Rnd: *K27 (31, 36, 41, 45, 50, 55), M1, K2, M1, K10, M1, K10, M1, K2, M1, K27 (31, 36, 41, 45, 50, 55), PM; rep from * to end. 166 (182, 202, 222, 238, 258, 278) sts.

Shape Armholes
*K to 2 (4, 4, 5, 5, 6, 6) sts before M, BO 4 (8, 8, 10, 10, 12, 12) sts; rep from * once more. 79 (83, 93, 101, 109, 117, 127) sts rem for each side. Remove Ms.

Back

Row 1 (RS): Work Chart A over 22 (24, 29, 33, 37, 41, 46) sts, work Chart B over 10 sts, work Chart C over 15 sts, work Chart D over 10 sts, work Chart A over 22 (24, 29, 33, 37, 41, 46) sts.

Row 2 (WS): Work Row 2 of charts in pattern as established.

Sizes 44", 48", 52" & 56" Only

Starting with next RS row, BO - (-, -, 2, 3, 4, 5) sts at beginning of next two rows. 79 (83, 93, 97, 103, 109, 117) sts.

All Sizes Resume

Dec Row (RS): K1, SSK, work in pattern to last 3 sts, K2tog, K1. 2 sts dec. 77 (81, 91, 95, 101, 107, 115) sts.

Cont to work as established, and rep Dec Row every RS row 0 (1, 3, 3, 5, 5, 7) more times. 77 (79, 85, 89, 91, 97, 101) sts. When armhole measures 7.5 (7.5, 8, 8.5, 9, 10, 11)", end with a WS row. Make a note of last row of Chart A worked. From this point on, work Chart A in St st to end of back.

Shape Shoulders

Short Row 1 (RS): Work in pattern as established until 11 (11, 12, 13, 13, 14, 14) sts remain, work GSR.

Short Row 2 (WS): Rep Row 1.

Short Row 3: Work in pattern until 22 (22, 24, 25, 25, 27, 28) sts remain, work GSR.

Short Row 4: Rep Row 3.

Short Row 5: Work in pattern to end, treating double sts as 1 st.

Row 6: BO 22 (22, 24, 25, 25, 27, 28) sts, work in pattern to end, treating double sts as 1 st.

Row 7: BO 22 (22, 24, 25, 25, 27, 28) sts, work in pattern across center 33 (35, 37, 39, 41, 43, 45) sts.

Row 8: Work in pattern to end.

BO all sts in pattern on next RS row.

Front

Rejoin yarn to begin a RS row, and work same as back until armhole measures 6.25 (6.25, 6.75, 7.25, 7.25, 8.25, 9.25)", ending with a WS row.

Shape Neck

Row 1 (RS): Work in pattern as established across 31 (31, 33, 35, 35, 38, 39) sts, join second ball and BO center 15 (17, 19, 19, 21, 21, 23) sts, work in pattern to end.

Row 2 (WS): Working both shoulders at the same time, work in pattern to end.

Row 3: Work in pattern across left shoulder to neck opening; with second ball, K2tog, BO 1 st, K2tog, BO 2 sts, work in pattern to end. 26 (26, 28, 30, 30, 33, 34) sts on right shoulder.

Row 4: Work in pattern across right shoulder to neck opening; with first ball, P2tog, BO 1 st, P2tog, BO 2 sts, work in pattern to end. 26 (26, 28, 30, 30, 33, 34) sts on each shoulder. Continuing to work in pattern, beginning with next row, BO 4 (4, 4, 5, 5, 4, 4) sts from each neck edge once, BO 0 (0, 0, 0, 0, 2, 2) sts from each neck edge once. 22 (22, 24, 25, 25, 27, 28) sts per shoulder.

When armhole measures same as back, end with same Chart row as back.

From this point on, work Chart A in St st to end of front.

Shape Shoulders

Short Row 1 (RS): Work in pattern across left shoulder; work in pattern across right shoulder until 11 (11, 12, 13, 13, 14, 14) sts remain, work GSR.

Short Row 2 (WS): Work in pattern across right shoulder; work in pattern across left shoulder until 11 (11, 12, 13, 13, 14, 14) st remain, work GSR.

Short Row 3: Work in pattern across left shoulder; work in pattern across right shoulder to end, treating double sts as 1 st.

Row 4: BO all right shoulder sts P-wise; P across left shoulder to end, treating the double sts as 1 st.

Row 5: BO all left shoulder sts K-wise.

Sleeves (make two the same)

Cuff

With preferred needles for working small circumferences, CO 46 sts. Distribute sts evenly around DPNs if using, PM, join in the rnd, careful not to twist.

Note: Work following charts in the rnd, working each row of chart from right to left.

Rnd 1: Work Chevron—Left chart over 4 sts, work Chevron Rib chart twice over center 38 sts, work Chevron—Right chart over 4 sts.

Cont to work charts as established; rep until cuff measures approx 4", ending with a chart Rnd 4.

Main Sleeve

Inc Rnd: K1, M1L, work in St st to last st, M1R, K1. 48 sts.

Cont to work in St st and rep Inc Rnd every 13 (9, 7, 5, 5, 4, 4) rnds 6 (3, 3, 7, 16, 10, 21) times, then every 0 (10, 8, 6, 0, 5, 0) rnds 0 (5, 7, 7, 0, 8, 0) times. 60 (64, 68, 76, 80, 84, 90) sts. When sleeve measures 17 (17, 17, 17, 17.5, 17.5, 18)", work in Garter Ridge for six rnds.

Size 32" Only

Dec Rnd: K29, K2tog, K to end. 59 sts.

Sizes 36", 40", 44", 48", 52" & 56" Only

Inc Rnd: K- (32, 34, 38, 40, 42, 45) M1L, K to end. - (65, 69, 77, 81, 85, 91) sts. 1 st inc.

Shape Armholes

Setup Rnd: K until 2 (4, 4, 5, 5, 6, 6) sts remain before M, BO 4 (8, 8, 10, 10, 12, 12) sts. 55 (57, 61, 67, 71, 73, 79) sts. Sleeve is now worked flat. Final BO st is passed over first st of next row.

Row 1 (RS): K3 (4, 6, 9, 11, 12, 15), P2, work Row 1 of Chart C over 15 sts, P1, PM, (P1, K1) six times, P1, PM, P1, work Row 1 of Chart C over 15 sts, P2, K3 (4, 6, 9, 11, 12, 15).

Row 2 (WS): P3 (4, 6, 9, 11, 12, 15), K2, work Row 2 of Chart C over 15 sts, K1, SM, K1, (P1, K1) six times, SM, K1, work Row 2 of Chart C over 15 sts, K2, P3 (4, 6, 9, 11, 12, 15).

Sizes 44", 48", 52" & 56" Only

Starting with next RS row, BO - (-, -, 3, 3, 3, 3) sts at beginning of next two rows. 55 (57, 61, 61, 65, 67, 73) sts.

St. Martin's Guernsey

Shape Sleeve Cap
Cont to work in pattern as established for two rows.
BO 1 st at beginning of next 30 (30, 34, 38, 42, 40, 44) rows.
25 (27, 27, 23, 23, 27, 29) sts.

Sizes 36" & 40" Only
BO 2 sts at beginning of next - (2, 2, -, -, -, -) rows. - (23, 23, -, -, -, -) sts.

Sizes 32", 52" & 56" Only
Dec Row (RS): K1, SSK, work in pattern to last 3 sts, K2tog, K1. 2 sts dec.
Rep Dec Row every RS row 0 (-, -, -, -, 1, 2) more times. 23 sts.
Work one WS row.

All Sizes Resume
BO 2 sts at beginning of next two rows.
BO 3 sts at beginning of next two rows. 13 sts.

Saddle
Change to smaller needles and cont to work 1x1 Rib, beginning and ending with a P st on RS rows, over remaining 13 sts, until saddle measures 4.5 (4.5, 5, 5.25, 5.25, 5.5, 5.75)" when stretched just slightly. Place saddle sts on holder.

Finishing
Block all pieces to measurements in schematic, stretching ribbing on sleeve upper arm and saddle as needed.
Set in sleeves and sew front edge of saddles to front shoulder sts. Set in back shoulders and sew sides of 2-row extension of back to first and second ribbing sts of saddle.
11 sts remain on saddle.

Neckband
With smaller circular needles, begin at back of left shoulder saddle, and transfer 11 saddle sts from holder to needle. Cont working in 1x1 Rib across 11 sts, PU and K 39 (41, 45, 47, 55, 57, 59) sts around front, maintain 1x1 Rib pattern across right saddle, PU and K 31 (33, 35, 37, 39, 41, 43) sts across back.
92 (96, 102, 106, 116, 120, 124) sts.
Join in the rnd, careful not to twist. Work 1x1 Rib until neck measures 4".
Using Kitchener Rib Bind Off, BO all sts loosely.
Weave in yarn ends.

A 32 (36, 40, 44, 48, 52, 56)"
B 27 (27, 28.5, 29, 29.5, 31.5, 32.5)"
C 17 (17, 18, 18, 18, 19, 19)"
D 7.5 (7.5, 8, 8.5, 9, 10, 11)"
E 15 (15.5, 16.5, 17.5, 18, 19, 20)"
F 4.5 (4.5, 5, 5.25, 5.25, 5.5, 5.75)"
G 6.25 (6.5, 7, 7.5, 8, 8.5, 9)"
H 3"
I 4.5 (4.5, 5, 5.25, 5.25, 5.5, 5.75)"
J 5.5 (5.5, 6, 6.5, 7, 8, 9)"
K 18 (18, 18, 18, 18.5, 19, 19)"
L 9.75"
M 13 (13.5, 14.5, 16, 17, 18, 19)"

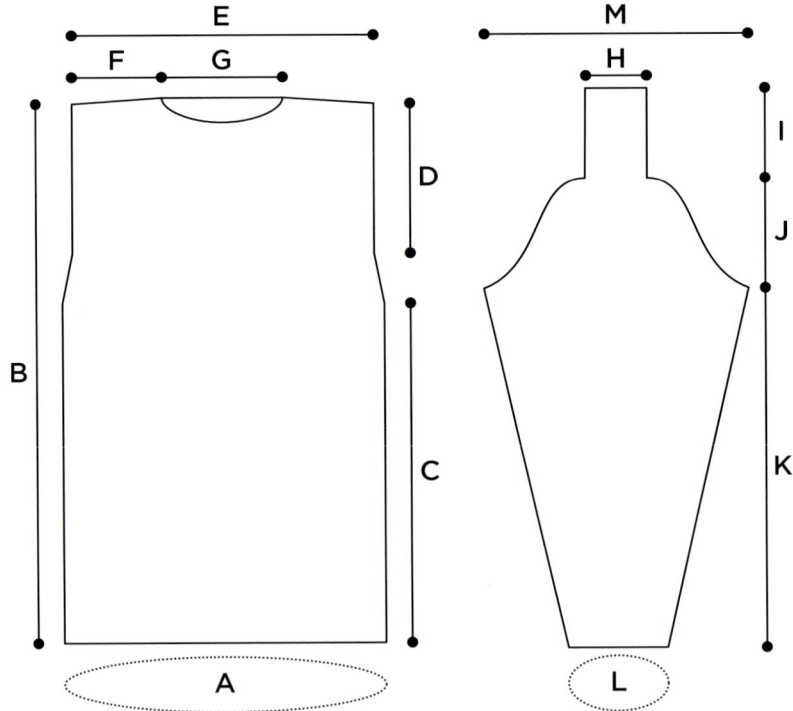

LEGEND

☐ **K**
RS: Knit stitch
WS: Purl stitch

• **P**
RS: Purl stitch
WS: Knit stitch

 **Cable 3 Over 3 Right (3/3 RC)**
Sl3 to CN, hold in back; K3, K3 from CN

Cable 3 Over 3 Left (3/3 LC)
Sl3 to CN, hold in front; K3, K3 from CN

Chevron—Left

Chevron—Right

Chevron Rib

Chart A

Chart B

Chart C

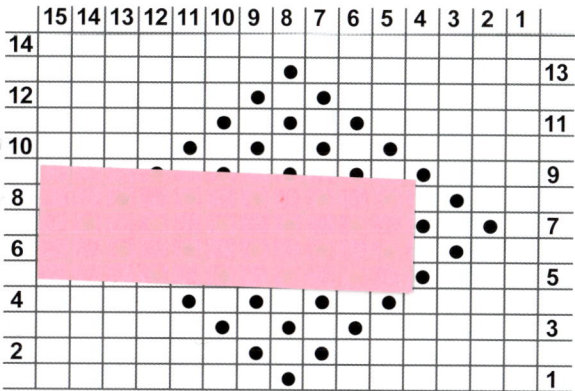

Chart D

St. Martin's Guernsey 95

Glossary

Common Stitches & Techniques

Slipped Stitches (Sl)
Always slip stitches purl-wise with yarn held to the wrong side of work, unless noted otherwise in the pattern.

Make 1 Left-Leaning Stitch (M1L)
Inserting LH needle from front to back, PU the horizontal strand between the st just worked and the next st, and K TBL.

Make 1 Right-Leaning Stitch (M1R)
Inserting LH needle from back to front, PU the horizontal strand between the st just worked and the next st, and K TFL.

Slip, Slip, Knit (SSK)
(Sl1 K-wise) twice; insert LH needle into front of these 2 sts and knit them together.

Centered Double Decrease (CDD)
Slip first and second sts together as if to work K2tog; K1; pass 2 slipped sts over the knit st.

Stockinette Stitch (St st, flat over any number of sts)
Row 1 (RS): Knit all sts.
Row 2 (WS): Purl all sts.
Rep Rows 1-2 for pattern.
St st in the round: Knit every rnd.

Garter Stitch (in the round over any number of sts)
Rnd 1: Purl all sts.
Rnd 2: Knit all sts.
Rep Rnds 1-2 for pattern.
Garter Stitch flat: Knit every row.
(One Garter ridge is comprised of two rows/rnds.)

1x1 Rib (flat or in the round, over an even number of sts)
Row/Rnd 1: (K1, P1) to end of row/rnd.
Rep Row/Rnd 1 for pattern.

2x2 Rib (flat over a multiple of 4 sts plus 2)
Row 1 (RS): K2, (P2, K2) to end of row.
Row 2 (WS): P2, (K2, P2) to end of row.
Rep Rows 1-2 for pattern.

2x2 Rib (in the round over a multiple of 4 sts)
Rnd 1: (K2, P2) to end of rnd.
Rep Rnd 1 for pattern.

Magic Loop Technique
A technique using one long circular needle to knit in the round around a small circumference. A tutorial can be found at https://tutorials.knitpicks.com/wptutorials/magic-loop.

Knitting in the Round with Two Circular Needles
A technique using two long circulars to knit around a small circumference. A tutorial can be found at https://tutorials.knitpicks.com/knitting-in-the-round-with-2-circular-needles.

Backward Loop Cast On
A simple, all-purpose cast on that can be worked mid-row. Also called Loop, Single, or E-Wrap Cast On. A tutorial can be found at https://tutorials.knitpicks.com/loop-cast-on.

Long Tail Cast On
Fast and neat once you get the hang of it. Also referred to as the Slingshot Cast On. A tutorial can be found at https://tutorials.knitpicks.com/long-tail-cast-on.

Cabled Cast On
A strong and nice looking basic cast on that can be worked mid-project. A tutorial can be found at https://tutorials.knitpicks.com/cabled-cast-on.

3-Needle Bind Off
Used to easily seam two rows of live stitches together. A tutorial can be found at https://tutorials.knitpicks.com/3-needle-bind-off.

Abbreviations

approx	approximately	KFB	knit into front and back of stitch	PSSO	pass slipped stitch over	SSP	slip, slip, purl these 2 stitches together through back loop
BO	bind off	K-wise	knit-wise	PU	pick up		
BOR	beginning of round	LH	left hand	P-wise	purl-wise	SSSK	slip, slip, slip, knit these 3 stitches together (like SSK)
CN	cable needle	M	marker	rep	repeat		
C (1, 2…)	color (1, 2…)	M1	make 1 stitch	Rev St st	reverse stockinette stitch	St st	stockinette stitch (*see above*)
CC	contrast color	M1L	make 1 left-leaning stitch (*see above*)	RH	right hand	st(s)	stitch(es)
CDD	centered double decrease (*see above*)	M1R	make 1 right-leaning stitch (*see above*)	rnd(s)	round(s)	TBL	through back loop
				RS	right side	TFL	through front loop
CO	cast on	MC	main color	Sk	skip	tog	together
cont	continue	P	purl	SK2P	slip 1, knit 2 together, pass slipped stitch over	W&T	wrap & turn (for short rows; *see next pg*)
dec(s)	decrease(es)	P2tog	purl 2 stitches together				
DPN(s)	double pointed needle(s)	P3tog	purl 3 stitches together	SKP	slip, knit, pass slipped stitch over	WE	work even
inc(s)	increase(s)			Sl	slip (*see above*)	WS	wrong side
K	knit	PM	place marker	SM	slip marker	WYIB	with yarn in back
K2tog	knit 2 stitches together	PFB	purl into front and back of stitch	SSK	slip, slip, knit these 2 stitches together (*see above*)	WYIF	with yarn in front
K3tog	knit 3 stitches together					YO	yarn over

Cabling Without a Cable Needle
A tutorial can be found at https://tutorials.knitpicks.com/learn-to-cable-without-a-cable-needle.

Felted Join (to splice yarn)
One method for joining a new length of yarn to the end of one that is already being used. A tutorial can be found at https://tutorials.knitpicks.com/felted-join.

Mattress Stitch
A neat, invisible seaming method that uses the bars between the first and second stitches on the edges. A tutorial can be found at https://tutorials.knitpicks.com/mattress-stitch.

Provisional Cast On (crochet method)
Used to cast on stitches that are also a row of live stitches, so they can be put onto a needle and used later.
Directions: Using a crochet hook, make a slipknot, then hold knitting needle in left hand, hook in right. With yarn in back of needle, work a chain st by pulling yarn over needle and through chain st. Move yarn back to behind needle, and rep for the number of sts required. Chain a few more sts off the needle, then break yarn and pull end through last chain. (CO sts may be incorrectly mounted; if so, work into backs of these sts.) To unravel later (when sts need to be picked up), pull chain end out; chain should unravel, leaving live sts. A video tutorial can be found at https://tutorials.knitpicks.com/crocheted-provisional-cast-on.

Provisional Cast On (crochet chain method)
Same result as the crochet method above, but worked differently, so you may prefer one or the other.
Directions: With a crochet hook, use scrap yarn to make a slipknot and chain the number of sts to be cast on, plus a few extra sts. Insert tip of knitting needle into first bump of crochet chain. Wrap project yarn around needle as if to knit, and pull yarn through crochet chain, forming first st. Rep this process until you have cast on the correct number of sts. To unravel later (when sts need to be picked up), pull chain out, leaving live sts. A photo tutorial can be found at https://tutorials.knitpicks.com/crocheted-provisional-cast-on.

Judy's Magic Cast On
This method creates stitches coming out in opposite directions from a seamless center line, perfect for starting toe-up socks.
Directions: Make a slipknot and place loop around one of the two needles; anchor loop counts as first st. Hold needles tog, with needle that yarn is attached to on top. In other hand, hold yarn so tail goes over index finger and yarn attached to ball goes over thumb. Bring tip of bottom needle over strand of yarn on finger (top strand), around and under yarn and back up, making a loop around needle. Pull loop snug. Bring top needle (with slipknot) over yarn tail on thumb (bottom strand), around and under yarn and back up, making a loop around needle. Pull loop snug. Cont casting on sts until desired number is reached; top yarn strand always wraps around bottom needle, and bottom yarn strand always wraps around top needle. A tutorial can be found at https://tutorials.knitpicks.com/judys-magic-cast-on.

Stretchy Bind Off
Directions: K2, *insert LH needle into front of 2 sts on RH needle and knit them tog—1 st remains on RH needle. K1; rep from * until all sts have been bound off. A tutorial can be found at https://tutorials.knitpicks.com/go-your-own-way-socks-toe-up-part-7-binding-off.

Jeny's Surprisingly Stretchy Bind Off (for 1x1 Rib)
Directions: Reverse YO, K1, pass YO over; *YO, P1, pass YO and previous st over P1; reverse YO, K1, pass YO and previous st over K1; rep from * until 1 st is left, then break working yarn and pull it through final st to complete BO.

Kitchener Stitch (also called Grafting)
Seamlessly join two sets of live stitches together.
Directions: With an equal number of sts on two needles, break yarn leaving a tail approx four times as long as the row of sts, and thread through a blunt yarn needle. Hold needles parallel with WSs facing in and both needles pointing to the right. Perform Step 2 on the first front st, then Step 4 on the first back st, then continue from Step 1, always pulling yarn tightly so the grafted row tension matches the knitted fabric:
Step 1: Pull yarn needle K-wise through front st and drop st from knitting needle.
Step 2: Pull yarn needle P-wise through next front st, leaving st on knitting needle.
Step 3: Pull yarn needle P-wise through first back st and drop st from knitting needle.
Step 4: Pull yarn needle K-wise through next back st, leaving st on knitting needle.
Rep Steps 1-4 until all sts have been grafted together, finishing by working Step 1 through the last remaining front st, then Step 3 through the last remaining back st. A tutorial can be found at https://tutorials.knitpicks.com/kitchener-stitch.

Short Rows
There are several options for how to handle short rows, so you may see different suggestions/intructions in a pattern.

Wrap and Turn (W&T) (one option for Short Rows)
Work until the st to be wrapped. If knitting: Bring yarn to front, Sl next st P-wise, return yarn to back; turn work, and Sl wrapped st onto RH needle. Cont across row. If purling: Bring yarn to back of work, Sl next st P-wise, return yarn to front; turn work and Sl wrapped st onto RH needle. Cont across row.
Picking up Wraps: Work to wrapped st. If knitting: Insert RH needle under wrap, then through wrapped st K-wise; K st and wrap tog. If purling: Sl wrapped st P-wise onto RH needle, use LH needle to lift wrap and place it onto RH needle; Sl wrap and st back onto LH needle, and P tog.
A tutorial for W&T can be found at https://tutorials.knitpicks.com/short-rows-wrap-and-turn-or-wt.

German Short Rows (another option for Short Rows)
Work to turning point; turn. WYIF, Sl first st P-wise. Bring yarn over back of right needle, pulling firmly to create a "double stitch" on RH needle. If next st is a K st, leave yarn at back; if next st is a P st, bring yarn to front between needles. When it's time to work into double st, knit both strands tog.

THIS COLLECTION FEATURES

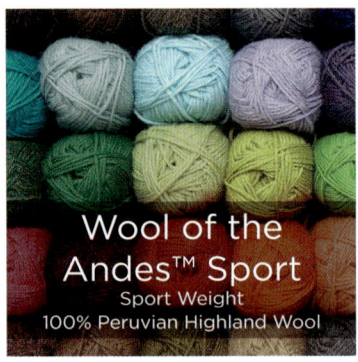
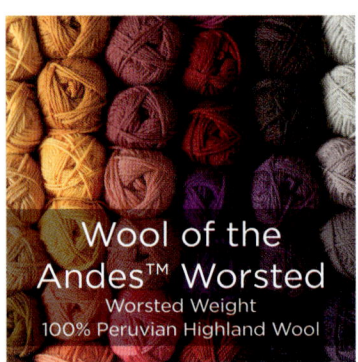

View these beautiful yarns and more at www.KnitPicks.com

Knit Picks yarn is both luxe and affordable—a seeming contradiction trounced! But it's not just about the pretty colors; we also care deeply about fiber quality and fair labor practices, leaving you with a gorgeously reliable product you'll turn to time and time again.